God is faithful
ALL His promises!

Love, Aunty Alem ♡

2015

Secret
for a
Successful Day

By
Alemla Zwahr

Table Of Contents

Dedication

*T*o my dad, Mr. Onen Jamir, and in loving memory of my mom, Mrs. Chubala Pongen, who have profoundly influenced my walk with the Lord. They have bequeathed to me as a heritage their faithfulness, dedication, loving sacrifice, inspiring model of prayer, and thirst after God. My deepest gratitude is given to them for teaching me to love the written Word of God, and encouraging me to study.

To my wonderful son, Aaron, I appreciate your love and obedience. May you continue to grow in our Lord Jesus Christ. It is a joy to be your mother. Your value is immeasurable!

To my loving husband, Philip, thank you for your faithfulness, love, prayers, and for your support and encouragement. I am privileged to be your wife.

Foreword

*I*t is a distinct honor for me to write my recommendation of this book, "Secret for a Successful Day."

My endorsement of this fine devotional book comes from serving as Mrs. Alemla Zwahr's pastor and observing her own dedication and devotion to the Lord Jesus Christ.

It is a work from her heart in a very personal way, which she lives out day by day.

I am sure it will help bring you to a successful life, as you use it daily.

Rev. B.B. Hankins D.M
Senior Pastor
The Christian Center Church
West Columbia, Texas

Acknowledgements

*F*irst of all, I give all the glory and honor to almighty God for His Word, His unfailing love, His mercy, and His grace that is greater than all my sins. Without Him I can do nothing, but with Him I can do all things. Look what the Lord has done!

My eternal gratitude goes to all the American missionaries who sacrificed their lives to come to Nagaland, India, to bring the good news of Jesus Christ. Their sacrifice for the sake of Christ has brought life to our people. I am a fourth generation Christian, a fruit of their labor of love. I would have been lost for eternity without their commitment to, "Go ye into all the world and preach the gospel to every creature." Matthew 16:15. May the God of love, the creator of the universe, bless this nation for touching the world with the good news of Jesus Christ.

My deepest gratitude to Christ for the Nations, Dallas, Texas; Mr. and Mrs. C.C. Baker of Tyler, Texas; Dr. & Mrs. Senka Yaden of Tyler, Texas for making it possible for me to come to the United States. I will always remember your kindness and love toward me.

To Ruth Angulo Bomar, I thank you for mentoring me to live a godly life and for introducing me to the Believer's Voice of Victory. I heard Brother and Sister Copeland teaching on the importance of giving God's Word first place in our lives and finding out what belongs to us in the Bible, and that's exactly what I did. I want to thank Brother and Sister Copeland, for teaching me how to talk *the talk and walk the walk. As the Copelands say, "One Word from God can change your life forever!"*

To Pastor B.B. Hankins of The Christian Center, West Colombia, Texas, for your encouragement and support to print this book. You've got the biggest heart for lost souls! You are the only pastor I have ever known to be wheeled in to the church with a broken knee to preach. Nothing stops you from preaching the Gospel! You are a "mantle" from which I'm learning to never to quit, but to keep fighting the good fight of faith.

To Dr. & Mrs. Gene Frank, your ministry of mobilizing people for the Gospel has made a significant difference in my life. I'm grateful to God for you and deeply appreciate the privilege of sitting under your anointing.

To Chester and Nelda Zwahr, my in-laws, thank you for training your son to go in the way of the Lord. You have done your homework. And thank you for being such great grandparents to our son, Aaron.

To Mrs. Paula Buck, thank you for being my American mother, sister, and friend. When I was new in this country, you took me in, and loved me like one of your own children. You are never too busy to listen to me. I am honored to know that I am always welcome in your home. I can truly say you are a "friend that sticks closer than a brother." You are a person of incredible value to me!

To Marcy Bryan, Paula Buck, Carolyn Chafin, Irma Pingenot, Linda Richards, Linda Wilson, Nelda Zwahr, and my husband, Philip, I gratefully acknowledge my indebtedness for your valued counsel and assistance in preparing "Secret for a Successful Day." I appreciate the gracious servant spirit you all have demonstrated to me. Your involvement has its definite mark of excellence on "Secret for a Successful Day."

Author's Personal Note

I never intended to write a book. I only set out to find God and His relevance to my life as my parents lived and taught me.

My final conversation with my mother, before she went home to be with the Lord, really challenged my readiness to meet the Lord. I looked like a Christian, talked like a Christian, and even acted like a Christian, but there was no personal relationship with God. I lived my own life, made my own choices based upon my own wisdom, and overcame, based upon my own strength. I attended church, but I was so distracted by judging others, being offended, or being critical that the sermons often went in one ear and out the other. I read the Bible on occasion, but I did not really understand it, much less apply it to my life.

My deep hunger to know God more, my desire to teach my young son about God, and through a series of divine relationships, the Lord began to establish me in His Word. All my life I thought that it was the people around me who needed to change, "not me." But through the mirror of God's Word, I began to see that I was full of fear, rejection, anger, and hate. I was impatient, self-righteous, judgmental, critical, and much more. I began to study what the Bible said about forgiveness because of my own struggle with unforgiveness. I studied God's principles of faith and love because of my own problems with fear, doubt, hate, and anger.

Through my biblical studies, I started a study journal and wrote every scripture that would help me in given areas of my life. My journal fit perfectly in my purse and I carried it with me everywhere. I read it, prayed it, spoke it, and meditated on it.

The life-changing power of God's Word revolutionized my entire life. It was my security during times of financial crisis, my confidence in the face of a life-threatening report from the doctor, and my peace and comfort during tragic deaths in the family. It has been and continues to be a vital resource for walking through and overcoming the challenges of this life.

That study journal is now this book, "Secret for a Successful Day." This is not just another book, but it is a book that will change your life forever. This is God's Word: it has the same power to do in your life what it has done in mine.

The Word of God is daily bread. "Give us this day our daily bread" (Matthew 6:11). *If you are going to feed your physical body today, you must feed your Spirit. May you be enriched through the entrance of God's Word into your heart and find the same life-changing power I have found!*

The wisdom of God's Word is the "Secret for a Successful Day!

Alemla Zwahr

Suggestions for Use

This book has been especially designed to be portable. Take it with you everywhere you go. Use it to build up your spiritual strength. Learn the art of encouraging yourself in the Lord, through His Word. When circumstances arise in your life, I challenge you to first turn your heart to God's Word. When knowing God and spending time with Him is your goal, all of life's major decisions will be made clear to you.

Memorize and keep the Word always before you. Build up a reservoir of God's Word for wisdom, direction, instruction, strength, comfort, encouragement, hope, power to defeat the enemy, deliverance, to get blessed and to prosper spirit, soul, and body. When you build yourself up with God's Word, He will make you rise up on the wings of faith like an eagle!

"And you will go places you have never been,
Do things you have never done,
Say things you have never said,
Have things you have never had,
Preach Words you have never preached,
Dream dreams you have never dreamed,
Sing songs you have never sang,
See things you have never seen,
Meet people you have never met.
You will know your covenant with God,
His calling, Anointing and commitment for His purpose,

You will have His character,
You will have the courage to do all that He has called
You to do, if you stand firm on His promises
And maintain your confession."

Dr. Dale Gentry
Founder of Dale Gentry Ministries
Fort Worth, Texas

GOD'S WORD: A FIRM FOUNDATION

The Pre-eminence of God's Word

Knowing and standing firmly on the Word of God is our foundation because God's Word is eternal, and He honors His Word. With His Word, God created the heaven and the earth. He has given the Word to us for direction in life: to be a good husband, to be a good wife, to teach our children, and to be all that God has made us to be. God's Word must be the first and the final authority in our daily life.

> In the beginning was the Word, and the Word was with God, and the Word was God. The same was in the beginning with God. All things were made by Him; and without Him was not any thing made that was made.
>
> John 1:1-3

> By the word of the LORD were the heavens made; and all the host of them by the breath of his mouth. For he spake, and it was done; he commanded, and it stood fast.
>
> Psalm 33:6 & 9

The LORD by wisdom hath founded the earth; by understanding hath he established the heavens. By his knowledge the depths are broken up, and the clouds drop down the dew.

Proverbs 3:19-20

This book of the law shall not depart out of thy mouth; but thou shalt meditate therein day and night, that thou mayest observe to do according to all that is written therein: for then thou shalt make thy way prosperous, and then thou shalt have good success.

Joshua 1:8

Ask of me, and I will make the nations your inheritance, the ends of the earth your possession.

Psalm 2:8 (NIV)

In everything you do, put God first, and He will direct you and crown your effort with success.

Proverbs 3:6 (TLB)

Only be strong and very courageous; be careful to do according to all the law which Moses My servant commanded you; do not turn from it to the right or to the left, so that you may have success wherever you go.

Joshua 1:7 (NASB)

Commit thy works unto the LORD, and thy thoughts shall be established.

Proverbs 16:3

There is no wisdom and no understanding And no counsel against the LORD.

Proverbs 21:30 (NASB)

Uzziah was sixteen years old when he became king, and he reigned fifty-two years in Jerusalem; and his mother's name was Jechiliah of Jerusalem. He did right in the sight of the LORD according to all that his father Amaziah had done. He continued to seek God in the days of Zechariah, who had understanding through the vision of God; and as long as he sought the LORD, God prospered him.

2 Chronicles 26:3-5 (NASB)

Happy is the man that findeth wisdom, and the man that getteth understanding. For the merchandise of it is better than the merchandise of silver, and the gain thereof than fine gold. She is more precious than rubies: and all the things thou canst desire are not to be compared unto her. Length of days is in her right hand; and in her left hand riches and honour. Her ways are ways of pleasantness, and all her paths are peace. She is a tree of life to them that lay hold upon her: and happy is every one that retaineth her.

Proverbs 3:13-18

The entrance of thy words giveth light; it giveth understanding unto the simple.

Psalm 119:130

Through wisdom is an house builded; and by understanding it is established: And by knowledge shall the chambers be filled with all precious and pleasant riches.

Proverbs 24:3-4

I rejoice at Your word, As one who finds great spoil.

Psalm 119:162 (NASB)

And the Lord replied, "I myself will go with you and give you success."

Exodus 33:14 (TLB)

The Infallible Word of God

Find out why we should take God at His Word

Heaven and earth shall pass away: but my words shall not pass away.

Mark 13:31

Blessed be the LORD, that hath given rest unto his people Israel, according to all that he promised: there hath not failed one word of all his good promise, which he promised by the hand of Moses his servant.

1 Kings 8:56

Every word of God is pure: he is a shield unto them that put their trust in him.

Proverbs 30:5

For ever, O LORD, thy word is settled in heaven.

Psalm 119:89

The grass withereth, the flower fadeth: but the word of our God shall stand for ever.

Isaiah 40:8

For verily I say unto you, Till heaven and earth pass, one jot or one tittle shall in no wise pass from the law, till all be fulfilled.

Matthew 5:18

The words of the LORD are pure words: as silver tried in a furnace of earth, purified seven times.

Psalm 12:6

As for God, his way is perfect: the word of the LORD

is tried: he is a buckler to all those that trust in him.

Psalm 18:30

For my thoughts are not your thoughts, neither are your ways my ways, saith the LORD. For as the heavens are higher than the earth, so are my ways higher than your ways, and my thoughts than your thoughts. For as the rain cometh down, and the snow from heaven, and returneth not thither, but watereth the earth, and maketh it bring forth and bud, that it may give seed to the sower, and bread to the eater: So shall my word be that goeth forth out of my mouth: it shall not return unto me void, but it shall accomplish that which I please, and it shall prosper in the thing whereto I sent it.

Isaiah 55:8-11

...all His commandments are sure. They stand fast for ever and ever, and are done in truth and uprightness.

Psalm 111:7-8

I rejoice at thy word, as one that findeth great spoil.

Psalm 119:16

All scripture is given by inspiration of God, and is profitable for doctrine, for reproof, for correction, for instruction in righteousness: That the man of God may be perfect, thoroughly furnished unto all good works.

2 Timothy 3:16-17

For the word of God is quick, and powerful, and sharper than any two-edged sword, piercing even to the dividing asunder of soul and spirit, and of the joints and marrow, and is a discerner of the thoughts and intents of the heart.

Hebrews 4:12

Thy word is a lamp unto my feet, and a light unto my path.

Psalm 119:105

Thy word have I hid in mine heart, that I might not sin against thee.

Psalm 119:11

And thine ears shall hear a word behind thee, saying, This is the way, walk ye in it, when ye turn to the right hand, and when ye turn to the left.

Isaiah 30:21

When thou goest, it shall lead thee; when thou sleepest, it shall keep thee; and when thou awakest, it shall talk with thee. For the commandment is a lamp; and the law is light; and reproofs of instruction are the way of life:

Proverbs 6:22-23

Thy testimonies also are my delight and my counselors.

Psalm 119:24

But the word of the Lord endureth for ever. And this is the word which by the gospel is preached unto you.

1 Peter 1:25

I am the LORD: I will speak, and the word that I shall speak shall come to pass; it shall be no more prolonged: for in your days,... will I say the word, and will perform it, saith the Lord GOD.

Ezekiel 12:25

As he spake by the mouth of his holy prophets, which have been since the world began: To give light to them that sit in darkness and in the shadow of death, to guide our feet into the way of peace.

Luke 1:70 & 79

For the mountains shall depart, and the hills be removed; but my kindness shall not depart from thee, neither shall the covenant of my peace be removed, saith the LORD that hath mercy on thee.

Isaiah 54:10

Then said Jesus to those Jews which believed on him, If ye continue in my word, then are ye my disciples indeed; And ye shall know the truth, and the truth shall make you free.

John 8:31-32

Search the scriptures; for in them ye think ye have eternal life: and they are they which testify of me.

John 5:39

...the words that I speak unto you, they are spirit, and they are life.

John 6:63

Then said the LORD unto me, Thou hast well seen: for I will hasten my word to perform it.

Jeremiah 1:12

For Ye are my witnesses, saith the LORD, and my servant whom I have chosen: that ye may know and believe me, and understand that I am he: before me there was no God formed, neither shall there be after me. I, even I, am the LORD; and beside me there is no saviour. I have declared, and have saved, and I have shewed, when there was no strange god among you: therefore ye are my witnesses, saith the LORD, that I am God. Yea, before the day was I am he; and there is none that can deliver out of my hand: I will work, and who shall let it?

Isaiah 43:10-13

Is not my word like as a fire? saith the LORD; and like a hammer that breaketh the rock in pieces?

Jeremiah 23:29

I will worship toward thy holy temple, and praise thy name for thy lovingkindness and for thy truth: for thou hast magnified thy word above all thy name.

Psalm 138:2

For all the promises of God in him are yea, and in him Amen, unto the glory of God by us.

2 Corinthians 1:20

God is not a man, that he should lie, nor a son of man, that he should change his mind. Does he speak and then not act? Does he promise and not fulfill?

Numbers 23:19 (NIV)

"To whom would you liken Me And make Me equal and compare Me, That we would be alike? "Those who lavish gold from the purse And weigh silver on the scale. Hire a goldsmith, and he makes it into a god; They bow down, indeed they worship it. "They lift it upon the shoulder and carry it; They set it in its place and it stands there. It does not move from its place. Though one may cry to it, it cannot answer; It cannot deliver him from his distress. "Remember this, and be assured; Recall it to mind, you transgressors. "Remember the former things long past, For I am God, and there is no other; I am God, and there is no one like Me, Declaring the end from the beginning, And from ancient times things which have not been done, Saying, 'My purpose will be established, And I will accomplish all My good pleasure'; Calling a bird of prey from the east, the man of My purpose from a far country. Truly I have spoken; truly I will bring it to pass. I have planned it, surely I will do it.

Isaiah 46:5-11 (NASB)

Walking in the Victory of Christ

The greatest defeat for the devil is to see Christians walking in victory. We cannot walk in victory until we find out who we are in Christ. The death, burial, and resurrection of our Lord Jesus Christ has made full provision for believers to live a victorious life. It is very important to find out what Christ has done for us and learn to see ourselves as God sees us.

Blessed be the God and Father of our Lord Jesus Christ, who has blessed us with every spiritual blessing in the heavenly places in Christ, just as He chose us in Him before the foundation of the world, that we would be holy and blameless before Him. In love He predestined us to adoption as sons through Jesus Christ to Himself, according to the kind intention of His will, to the praise of the glory of His grace, which He freely bestowed on us in the Beloved. In Him we have redemption through His blood, the forgiveness of our trespasses, according to the riches of His grace which He lavished on us. In all wisdom and insight He made known to us the mystery of His will, according to His kind intention which He purposed in Him with a view to an administration suitable to the fullness of the times, that is, the summing up of all things in Christ, things in the heavens and things on the earth. In Him also we have obtained an inheritance, having been predestined according to His purpose who works all things after the counsel of His will, to the end that we who were the first to hope in Christ would be to the praise of His glory. In Him, you also, after listening to the message of truth, the gospel of your salvation— having also believed, you were sealed in Him with the Holy Spirit of promise, who is given as a pledge of our inheritance, with a view to the redemption of God's own possession, to the praise of His glory.

Ephesians 1:3-14 (NASB)

For we are his workmanship, created in Christ Jesus unto good works, which God hath before ordained that we should walk in them.

Ephesians 2:10

Knowing that a man is not justified by the works of the law, but by the faith of Jesus Christ, even we have believed in Jesus Christ, that we might be justified by the faith of Christ, and not by the works of the law: for by the works of the law shall no flesh be justified.

Galatians 2:16

For whatsoever is born of God overcometh the world: and this is the victory that overcometh the world, even our faith. Who is he that overcometh the world, but he that believeth that Jesus is the Son of God?

1 John 5:4-5

Therefore if any man be in Christ, he is a new creature: old things are passed away; behold, all things are become new.

2 Corinthians 5:17

For he hath made him to be sin for us, who knew no sin; that we might be made the righteousness of God in him.

2 Corinthians 5:21

I write unto you, little children, because your sins are forgiven you for his name's sake.

1 John 2:12

Wherefore thou art no more a servant, but a son; and if a son, then an heir of God through Christ.

Galatians 4:7

For ye are all the children of God by faith in Christ Jesus. For as many of you as have been baptized into Christ have put on Christ.

Galatians 3:26-27

Even the righteousness of God through faith in Jesus Christ for all those who believe; for there is no distinction; for all have sinned and fall short of the glory of God, being justified as a gift by His grace through the redemption which is in Christ Jesus;

Romans 3:22-24 (NASB)

But of him are ye in Christ Jesus, who of God is made unto us wisdom, and righteousness, and sanctification, and redemption:

1 Corinthians 1:30

There is therefore now no condemnation to them which are in Christ Jesus, who walk not after the flesh, but after the Spirit. For the law of the Spirit of life in Christ Jesus hath made me free from the law of sin and death.

Romans 8:1-2

For the wages of sin is death; but the gift of God is eternal life through Jesus Christ our Lord.

Romans 6:23

Being born again, not of corruptible seed, but of incorruptible, by the word of God, which liveth and abideth for ever.

1 Peter 1:23

For as in Adam all die, even so in Christ shall all be made alive.

1 Corinthians 15:22

But ye are a chosen generation, a royal priesthood, an holy nation, a peculiar people; that ye should shew forth the praises of him who hath called you out of darkness into his marvelous light:

1 Peter 2:9

As ye have therefore received Christ Jesus the Lord, so walk ye in him: Rooted and built up in him, and stablished in the faith, as ye have been taught, abounding therein with thanksgiving.

Colossians 2:6-7

But whatever things were gain to me, those things I have counted as loss for the sake of Christ. More than that, I count all things to be loss in view of the surpassing value of knowing Christ Jesus my Lord, for whom I have suffered the loss of all things, and count them but rubbish so that I may gain Christ, And may be found in Him, not having a righteousness of my own derived from the Law, but that which is through faith in Christ, the righteousness which comes from God on the basis of faith, that I may know Him and the power of His resurrection and the fellowship of His sufferings, being conformed to His death; in order that I may attain to the resurrection from the dead. Not that I have already obtained it or have already become perfect, but I press on so that I may lay hold of that for which also I was laid hold of by Christ Jesus. Brethren, I do not regard myself as having laid hold of it yet; but one thing I do: forgetting what lies behind and reaching forward to what lies ahead, I press on toward the goal for the prize of the upward call of God in Christ Jesus. Let us therefore, as many as are perfect, have this attitude; and if in anything you have a different attitude, God will reveal that also to you; However, let us keep living by that same standard to which we have attained.

Philippians 3:7-16 (NASB)

Be ye therefore followers of God, as dear children;

Ephesians 5:1

And you, being dead in your sins and the uncircumcision of your flesh, hath he quickened together with him, having forgiven you all trespasses;

Colossians 2:13

Likewise reckon ye also yourselves to be dead indeed unto sin, but alive unto God through Jesus Christ our Lord.

Romans 6:11

Because it is written, Be ye holy; for I am holy.

1 Peter 1:16

I am crucified with Christ: nevertheless I live; yet not I, but Christ liveth in me: and the life which I now live in the flesh I live by the faith of the Son of God, who loved me, and gave himself for me.

Galatians 2:20

We know that whosoever is born of God sinneth not; but he that is begotten of God keepeth himself, and that wicked one toucheth him not.

1 John 5:18

If ye then be risen with Christ, seek those things which are above, where Christ sitteth on the right hand of God. Set your affection on things above, not on things on the earth. For ye are dead, and your life is hid with Christ in God. When Christ, who is our life, shall appear, then shall ye also appear with him in glory.

Colossians 3:1-4

For I am not ashamed of the gospel of Christ: for it is the power of God unto salvation to every one that believeth; to the Jew first, and also to the Greek.

Romans 1:16

He that saith he abideth in him ought himself also so to walk, even as he walked.

1 John 2:6

Freedom From Sin and Addiction

Our bodies are not our own; God made us for His glory. We should ask Him to help us with our problem because there is no problem too hard for Him. He accepts us and loves us, no matter what we have done. God is a loving God, who wants to help us and is ready to receive us into His loving arms. He wants to set us free from the bondages of sin and addiction. He will help us to live a life that will bring glory to His name, if we will let Him.

But now being made free from sin, and become servants to God, ye have your fruit unto holiness, and the end everlasting life.

Romans 6:22

For ye are bought with a price: therefore glorify God in your body, and in your spirit, which are God's.

1 Corinthians 6:20

Stand fast therefore in the liberty wherewith Christ hath made us free, and be not entangled again with the yoke of bondage.

Galatians 5:1

Be not overcome of evil, but overcome evil with good.

Romans 12:21

He that walketh with wise men shall be wise: but a companion of fools shall be destroyed.

Proverbs 13:20

Then said Jesus unto his disciples, If any man will

come after me, let him deny himself, and take up his cross, and follow me.

Matthew 16:24

Know ye not that ye are the temple of God, and that the Spirit of God dwelleth in you? If any man defile the temple of God, him shall God destroy; for the temple of God is holy, which temple ye are.

1 Corinthians 3:16-17

But if from thence thou shalt seek the LORD thy God, thou shalt find him, if thou seek him with all thy heart and with all thy soul.

Deuteronomy 4:29

And the LORD passed by before him, and proclaimed, The LORD, The LORD God, merciful and gracious, longsuffering, and abundant in goodness and truth, Keeping mercy for thousands, forgiving iniquity and transgression and sin, and that will by no means clear the guilty; visiting the iniquity of the fathers upon the children, and upon the children's children, unto the third and to the fourth generation.

Exodus 34:6-7

But I am poor and needy; yet the Lord thinketh upon me: thou art my help and my deliverer; make no tarrying, O my God.

Psalm 40:17

And all things, whatsoever ye shall ask in prayer, believing, ye shall receive.

Matthew 21:22

Wait on the LORD: be of good courage, and he shall

strengthen thine heart: wait, I say, on the LORD.

Psalm 27:14

This poor man cried, and the LORD heard him, and saved him out of all his troubles.

Psalm 34:6

It is God that girdeth me with strength, and maketh my way perfect. He maketh my feet like hinds' feet, and setteth me upon my high places.

Psalm 18:32-33

God is our refuge and strength, a very present help in trouble.

Psalm 46:1

I have set the LORD always before me: because he is at my right hand, I shall not be moved. Therefore my heart is glad, and my glory rejoiceth: my flesh also shall rest in hope. For thou wilt not leave my soul in hell; neither wilt thou suffer thine Holy One to see corruption. Thou wilt shew me the path of life: in thy presence is fullness of joy; at thy right hand there are pleasures for evermore.

Psalm 16:8-11

He will regard the prayer of the destitute, and not despise their prayer.

Psalm 102:17

They cried unto thee, and were delivered: they trusted in thee, and were not confounded.

Psalm 22:5

But they that wait upon the LORD shall renew their

strength; they shall mount up with wings as eagles; they shall run, and not be weary; and they shall walk, and not faint.

Isaiah 40:31

Forsake me not, O LORD: O my God, be not far from me. Make haste to help me, O Lord my salvation.

Psalm 38:21-22

O my soul, thou hast said unto the LORD, Thou art my Lord: my goodness extendeth not to thee;

Psalm 16:2

Teach me thy way, O LORD, and lead me in a plain path, because of mine enemies.

Psalm 27:11

I will extol thee, O LORD; for thou hast lifted me up, and hast not made my foes to rejoice over me. O LORD my God, I cried unto thee, and thou hast healed me. O LORD, thou hast brought up my soul from the grave: thou hast kept me alive, that I should not go down to the pit. Sing unto the LORD, O ye saints of his, and give thanks at the remembrance of his holiness. For his anger endureth but a moment; in his favour is life: weeping may endure for a night, but joy cometh in the morning. And in my prosperity I said, I shall never be moved. LORD, by thy favour thou hast made my mountain to stand strong: thou didst hide thy face, and I was troubled. I cried to thee, O LORD; and unto the LORD I made supplication. What profit is there in my blood, when I go down to the pit? Shall the dust praise thee? shall it declare thy truth? Hear, O LORD, and have mercy upon me: LORD, be thou my helper. Thou hast turned for me my mourning into dancing: thou hast put off my sackcloth, and girded me with gladness; To the end that my glory may sing praise to thee, and not be silent. O LORD my God, I will give thanks unto thee for ever.

Psalm 30:1-12

I will instruct thee and teach thee in the way which thou shalt go: I will guide thee with mine eye.

Psalm 32:8

In You, O LORD, I have taken refuge; Let me never be ashamed; In Your righteousness deliver me. Incline Your ear to me, rescue me quickly; Be to me a rock of strength, A stronghold to save me. For You are my rock and my fortress; For Your name's sake You will lead me and guide me. You will pull me out of the net which they have secretly laid for me, For You are my strength. Into Your hand I commit my spirit; You have ransomed me, O LORD, God of truth. I hate those who regard vain idols, But I trust in the LORD. I will rejoice and be glad in Your lovingkindness, Because You have seen my affliction; You have known the troubles of my soul, And You have not given me over into the hand of the enemy; You have set my feet in a large place. Be gracious to me, O LORD, for I am in distress; My eye is wasted away from grief, my soul and my body also. For my life is spent with sorrow And my years with sighing; My strength has failed because of my iniquity, And my body has wasted away. Because of all my adversaries, I have become a reproach, Especially to my neighbors, And an object of dread to my acquaintances; Those who see me in the street flee from me. I am forgotten as a dead man, out of mind; I am like a broken vessel. For I have heard the slander of many, Terror is on every side;

While they took counsel together against me, They schemed to take away my life. But as for me, I trust in You, O LORD, I say, "You are my God." My times are in Your hand; Deliver me from the hand of my enemies and from those who persecute me. Make Your face to shine upon Your servant; Save me in Your lovingkindness. Let me not be put to shame, O LORD, for I call upon You; Let the wicked be put to shame, let them be silent in Sheol. Let the lying lips be mute, Which speak arrogantly against the Righteous with pride and contempt. How great is Your goodness, Which You have stored up for those who fear You, Which You have wrought for those who take refuge in You, Before the sons of men! You hide them in the secret place of Your presence from the conspiracies of man; You keep them secretly in a shelter from the strife of tongues. Blessed be the LORD, For He has made marvelous His lovingkindness to me in a besieged city. As for me, I said in my alarm, "I am cut off from before Your eyes"; Nevertheless You heard the voice of my supplications when I cried to You. O love the LORD, all you His godly ones! The LORD preserves the faithful And fully recompenses the proud doer. Be strong and let your heart take courage, All you who hope in the LORD.

Psalm 31:1-24 (NASB)

God setteth the solitary in families: he bringeth out those which are bound with chains: but the rebellious dwell in a dry land.

Psalm 68:6

I waited patiently for the LORD; and he inclined unto me, and heard my cry. He brought me up also out of an horrible pit, out of the miry clay, and set my feet upon a rock, and established my goings. And he hath put a new song in my mouth, even praise unto our God: many shall see it, and fear, and shall trust in the LORD. Blessed is that man that maketh the LORD his trust, and respecteth not the proud, nor such as turn aside to lies. Many, O LORD my God, are thy wonderful works which thou hast done, and thy thoughts which are to us-ward: they cannot be reckoned up in order unto thee: if I would declare and speak of them, they are more than can be numbered. I delight to do thy will, O my God: yea, thy law is within my heart.

Psalm 40:1-5 & 8

Withhold not thou thy tender mercies from me, O LORD: let thy lovingkindness and thy truth continually preserve me. Be pleased, O LORD, to deliver me: O LORD, make haste to help me.

Psalm 40:11 &13

The LORD redeemeth the soul of his servants: and none of them that trust in him shall be desolate.

Psalm 34:22

In thee, O LORD, do I put my trust: let me never be put to confusion. Deliver me in thy righteousness, and cause me to escape: incline thine ear unto me, and save me. Be thou my strong habitation, whereunto I may continually resort: thou hast given commandment to save me; for thou art my rock and my fortress. Deliver me, O my God, out of the hand of the wicked, out of the hand of the unrighteous and cruel man.

Psalm 71:1-4

Teach me thy way, O LORD; I will walk in thy truth:

unite my heart to fear thy name. I will praise thee, O Lord my God, with all my heart: and I will glorify thy name for evermore. For great is thy mercy toward me: and thou hast delivered my soul from the lowest hell.

Psalm 86:11-13

Unless thy law had been my delights, I should then have perished in mine affliction. I am thine, save me; for I have sought thy precepts.

Psalm 119:92 & 94

Let my cry come near before thee, O LORD: give me understanding according to thy word. Let my supplication come before thee: deliver me according to thy word. My lips shall utter praise, when thou hast taught me thy statutes. My tongue shall speak of thy word: for all thy commandments are righteousness. Let thine hand help me; for I have chosen thy precepts. I have longed for thy salvation, O LORD; and thy law is my delight. Let my soul live, and it shall praise thee; and let thy judgments help me. I have gone astray like a lost sheep; seek thy servant; for I do not forget thy commandments.

Psalm 119:169-176

In my distress I cried unto the LORD, and he heard me.

Psalm 120:1

And I will walk at liberty: for I seek thy precepts.

Psalm 119:45

Open to me the gates of righteousness: I will go into them, and I will praise the LORD:

Psalm 118:19

Through thy precepts I get understanding: therefore I
hate every false way.

Psalm 119:104

I have inclined mine heart to perform thy statutes
alway, even unto the end.

Psalm 119:112

The wilderness and the solitary place shall be glad
for them; and the desert shall rejoice, and blossom
as the rose. It shall blossom abundantly, and rejoice
even with joy and singing: the glory of Lebanon
shall be given unto it, the excellency of Carmel and
Sharon, they shall see the glory of the LORD, and
the excellency of our God. Strengthen ye the weak
hands, and confirm the feeble knees. Say to them
that are of a fearful heart, Be strong, fear not: behold,
your God will come with vengeance, even God with
a recompense; he will come and save you. Then the
eyes of the blind shall be opened, and the ears of the
deaf shall be unstopped. Then shall the lame man leap
as an hart, and the tongue of the dumb sing: for in
the wilderness shall waters break out, and streams
in the desert. And the parched ground shall become
a pool, and the thirsty land springs of water: in the
habitation of dragons, where each lay, shall be grass
with reeds and rushes. And an highway shall be there,
and a way, and it shall be called The way of holiness;
the unclean shall not pass over it; but it shall be for
those: the wayfaring men, though fools, shall not err
therein. No lion shall be there, nor any ravenous beast
shall go up thereon, it shall not be found there; but the
redeemed shall walk there: And the ransomed of the
LORD shall return, and come to Zion with songs and
everlasting joy upon their heads: they shall obtain joy

and gladness, and sorrow and sighing shall flee away.

Isaiah 35:1-10

Thy testimonies are wonderful: therefore doth my soul keep them. The entrance of thy words giveth light; it giveth understanding unto the simple. I opened my mouth, and panted: for I longed for thy commandments. Look thou upon me, and be merciful unto me, as thou usest to do unto those that love thy name. Order my steps in thy word: and let not any iniquity have dominion over me. Deliver me from the oppression of man: so will I keep thy precepts. Make thy face to shine upon thy servant; and teach me thy statutes.

Psalm 119:129-135

But I say, walk by the Spirit, and you will not carry out the desire of the flesh. For the flesh sets its desire against the Spirit, and the Spirit against the flesh; for these are in opposition to one another, so that you may not do the things that you please. But if you are led by the Spirit, you are not under the Law. Now the deeds of the flesh are evident, which are: immorality, impurity, sensuality, idolatry, sorcery, enmities, strife, jealousy, outbursts of anger, disputes, dissensions, factions, envying, drunkenness, carousing, and things like these, of which I forewarn you, just as I have forewarned you, that those who practice such things will not inherit the kingdom of God. But the fruit of the Spirit is love, joy, peace, patience, kindness, goodness, faithfulness, gentleness, self-control; against such things there is no law. Now those who belong to Christ Jesus have crucified the flesh with its passions and desires. If we live by the Spirit, let us also walk by the Spirit.

Galatians 5:16-25 (NASB)

Now the Lord is the Spirit, and where the Spirit of the Lord is, there is liberty. But we all, with unveiled face, beholding as in a mirror the glory of the Lord, are being transformed into the same image from glory to glory, just as from the Lord, the Spirit.

2 Corinthians 3:17-18 (NASB)

Forgiveness

God's Word tells us to forgive not seven times, but to forgive seventy times seven. We cannot live a victorious Christian life with unforgiveness and bitterness in our heart. As God forgives us, we must also learn to forgive one another.

Choosing to forgive does not remove the hurt. But God heals the hurt as we continue to choose to release the offence and the offender to Him.

It is not what other people do to us, but it is how we respond to their action that impacts our life.

Choosing not to forgive has a great impact on our life. Unforgiveness is like a deadly poison. We must simply refuse to let unforgiveness control our destiny.

To the Lord our God belong mercies and forgiveness, though we have rebelled against him;

Daniel 9:9

But there is forgiveness with thee, that thou mayest be feared.

Psalm 130:4

'The LORD is slow to anger and abundant in lovingkindness, forgiving iniquity and transgression; but He will by no means clear the guilty, visiting the iniquity of the fathers on the children to the third and the fourth generations.'

Numbers 14:18 (NASB)

Then said Jesus, Father, forgive them; for they know not what they do. And they parted his raiment, and cast lots.

Luke 23:34

The LORD Pardons and Rebukes, So the LORD said, "I have pardoned them according to your word;
Numbers 14:20 (NASB)

In Him we have redemption through His blood, the forgiveness of our trespasses, according to the riches of His grace
Ephesians 1:7 (NASB)

Blessed is he whose transgression is forgiven, whose sin is covered. Blessed is the man unto whom the LORD imputeth not iniquity, and in whose spirit there is no guile.
Psalm 32:1-2

As far as the east is from the west, so far hath he removed our transgressions from us.
Psalm 103:12

If we confess our sins, he is faithful and just to forgive us our sins, and to cleanse us from all unrighteousness.
1 John 1:9

In whom we have redemption through his blood, even the forgiveness of sins:
Colossians 1:14

I write unto you, little children, because your sins are forgiven you for his name's sake.
1 John 2:12

Forbearing one another, and forgiving one another, if any man have a quarrel against any: even as Christ forgave you, so also do ye.
Colossians 3:13

Judge not, and ye shall not be judged: condemn not, and ye shall not be condemned: forgive, and ye shall be forgiven:

Luke 6:37

And according to the Law, *one may* almost *say*, all things are cleansed with blood, and without shedding of blood there is no forgiveness.

Hebrews 9:22 (NASB)

Have mercy upon me, O God, according to thy lovingkindness: according unto the multitude of thy tender mercies blot out my transgressions.

Psalm 51:1

Endeavouring to keep the unity of the Spirit in the bond of peace. And be ye kind one to another, tenderhearted, forgiving one another, even as God for Christ's sake hath forgiven you.

Ephesians 4:3 & 32

And when ye stand praying, forgive, if ye have ought against any: that your Father also which is in heaven may forgive you your trespasses.

Mark 11:25

For if ye forgive men their trespasses, your heavenly Father will also forgive you: But if ye forgive not men their trespasses, neither will your Father forgive your trespasses.

Matthew 6:14-15

But that ye may know that the Son of man hath power upon earth to forgive sins...

Luke 5:24

Then came Peter to him, and said, Lord, how oft shall my brother sin against me, and I forgive him? till seven times? Jesus saith unto him, I say not unto thee, Until seven times: but, Until seventy times seven.

Matthew 18:21-22

Take heed to yourselves: If thy brother trespass against thee, rebuke him; and if he repent, forgive him. And if he trespass against thee seven times in a day, and seven times in a day turn again to thee, saying, I repent; thou shalt forgive him.

Luke 17:3-4

If I regard iniquity in my heart, the Lord will not hear me: But verily God hath heard me; he hath attended to the voice of my prayer. Blessed be God, which hath not turned away my prayer, nor his mercy from me.

Psalm 66:18-20

I said, LORD, be merciful unto me: heal my soul; for I have sinned against thee.

Psalm 41:4

Therefore if thou bring thy gift to the altar, and there rememberest that thy brother hath ought against thee; Leave there thy gift before the altar, and go thy way; first be reconciled to thy brother, and then come and offer thy gift.

Matthew 5:23-24

The sacrifices of God are a broken spirit: a broken and a contrite heart, O God, thou wilt not despise.

Psalm 51:17

If my people, which are called by my name, shall humble themselves, and pray, and seek my face, and turn from their wicked ways; then will I hear from heaven, and will forgive their sin, and will heal their land.

2 Chronicles 7:14

For I will be merciful to their unrighteousness, and their sins and their iniquities will I remember no more.

Hebrews 8:12

Be it known unto you therefore, men and brethren, that through this man is preached unto you the forgiveness of sins:

Acts 13:38

For thou, Lord, art good, and ready to forgive; and plenteous in mercy unto all them that call upon thee.

Psalm 86:5

Be not overcome of evil, but overcome evil with good.

Romans 12:2

Unquenchable Forces: Faith and Love

*Faith and love are the most foundational elements of our Christian walk. Without love we are nothing, "...*and if I have a faith that can move mountains, but have not love I am nothing," (1Corinthians 13:2). *Faith is equally important,* "And without faith it is impossible to please God..." (Hebrews 11:6) *faith is how we come to God; love is how we walk before man. Together, faith and love are unquenchable forces.*

For in Jesus Christ neither circumcision availeth any thing, nor uncircumcision; but faith which worketh by love.

Galatians 5:6

Faith

Now faith is the substance of things hoped for, the evidence of things not seen. For by it the elders obtained a good report. Through faith we understand that the worlds were framed by the word of God, so that things which are seen were not made of things which do appear. By faith Abel offered unto God a more excellent sacrifice than Cain, by which he obtained witness that he was righteous, God testifying of his gifts: and by it he being dead yet speaketh. By faith Enoch was translated that he should not see death; and was not found, because God had translated him: for before his translation he had this testimony, that he pleased God. But without faith it is impossible to please him: for he that cometh to God must believe that he is, and that he is a rewarder of them that diligently seek him. By faith Noah, being warned of God of things not seen as yet, moved with fear, prepared an ark to the saving of his house; by the which he condemned the world, and became heir of the righteousness which is by faith. By faith Abraham, when he was called to go out into a place which he should after receive for an inheritance, obeyed; and he went out, not knowing whither he went. By faith he sojourned in the land of promise, as in a strange country, dwelling in tabernacles with Isaac and Jacob, the heirs with him of the same promise: For he looked for a city which hath foundations, whose builder and maker is God. Through faith also Sara herself received strength to conceive seed, and was delivered of a child when she was past age, because she judged him faithful who had promised. Therefore sprang there even of one, and him as good as dead, so many as the stars of the sky in multitude, and as the sand which is by the sea shore innumerable. These all died in faith, not having received the promises, but having seen them afar off, and were persuaded of them, and embraced them, and confessed that they were strangers and pilgrims on the earth. For they that say such things declare plainly that they seek a country. And truly, if they had been mindful of that country from whence they came out, they might have had opportunity to have returned. But now they desire a better country, that is, an heavenly: wherefore God is not ashamed to be called their God: for he hath prepared for them a city. By faith Abraham, when he was tried, offered up Isaac: and he that had received the promises offered up his only begotten son, Of whom it was said, That in Isaac shall thy seed be called: Accounting that God was able to raise him up, even from the dead; from whence also he received him in a figure. By faith Isaac blessed Jacob and Esau concerning things to come. By faith Jacob, when he was a dying, blessed both the sons of Joseph; and worshipped, leaning upon the top of his staff. By faith Joseph, when he died, made mention of the departing of the children of Israel; and gave commandment concerning his bones. By faith Moses, when he was born, was hid three months of his parents, because they saw he was a proper child; and they were not afraid of the king's commandment. By faith Moses, when he was come to years, refused to be called the son of Pharaoh's daughter; Choosing rather to suffer affliction with the people of God, than to enjoy the pleasures of sin for a season; Esteeming the reproach of Christ greater riches than the treasures in Egypt: for he had respect unto the recompence of the reward. By faith he forsook Egypt, not fearing the wrath of the king: for he endured, as seeing him who is invisible. Through faith he kept the Passover, and the sprinkling of blood, lest he that destroyed the firstborn should touch them. By faith they passed through the Red Sea as by dry land: which the Egyptians assaying to do were drowned. By faith the walls of Jericho fell down, after they were compassed about seven days. By faith the harlot Rahab perished not with them that believed not, when she had received the spies with peace. And what shall I more say? for the time would fail me to tell of Gideon, and of Barak, and of Samson, and of Jephthae; of David also, and Samuel, and of the prophets: Who through faith subdued kingdoms, wrought righteousness, obtained promises, stopped the mouths of lions, Quenched the violence of fire, escaped the edge of the sword, out of weakness were made strong, waxed valiant in fight, turned to flight the armies of the aliens. Women received their dead raised to life again: and others were tortured, not accepting deliverance; that they might obtain a better resurrection: And others had trial of cruel mockings and scourgings, yea, moreover of bonds and imprisonment: They were stoned, they were sawn asunder, were tempted, were slain with the sword: they wandered about in sheepskins and goatskins; being destitute, afflicted, tormented; (Of whom the world was not worthy:) they wandered in deserts, and in mountains, and in dens and caves of the earth. And these all, having obtained a good report through faith, received not the promise: God having provided some better thing for us, that they without us should not be made perfect.

Hebrews 11:1-40 (NASB)

Therefore, since we have so great a cloud of witnesses surrounding us, let us also lay aside every encumbrance and the sin which so easily entangles us, and let us run with endurance the race that is set before us, fixing our eyes on Jesus, the author and perfecter of faith, who for the joy set before Him endured the cross, despising the shame, and has sat down at the right hand of the throne of God.

Hebrews 12:1-2 (NASB)

As ye have therefore received Christ Jesus the Lord, so walk ye in him: Rooted and built up in him, and stablished in the faith, as ye have been taught, abounding therein with thanksgiving.

Colossians 2:6-7

Seeing then that we have a great high priest, that is passed into the heavens, Jesus the Son of God, let us hold fast our profession.

Hebrews 4:14

So then faith cometh by hearing, and hearing by the word of God.

Romans 10:17

For therein is the righteousness of God revealed from faith to faith: as it is written, The just shall live by faith.

Romans 1:17

Knowing that a man is not justified by the works of the law, but by the faith of Jesus Christ, even we have believed in Jesus Christ, that we might be justified by the faith of Christ, and not by the works of the law: for by the works of the law shall no flesh be justified. For I through the law am dead to the law, that I might live unto God.

Galatians 2:16 & 19

(As it is written, I have made thee a father of many nations,) before him whom he believed, even God, who quickeneth the dead, and calleth those things which be not as though they were. He staggered not at the promise of God through unbelief; but was strong in faith, giving glory to God; And being fully persuaded that, what he had promised, he was able also to perform.

Romans 4:17 & 20-21

But that no man is justified by the law in the sight of God, it is evident: for, The just shall live by faith. That the blessing of Abraham might come on the Gentiles through Jesus Christ; that we might receive the promise of the Spirit through faith.

Galatians 3:11 & 14

For whatsoever is born of God overcometh the world: and this is the victory that overcometh the world, even our faith.

1 John 5:4

For we through the Spirit wait for the hope of righteousness by faith.

Galatians 5:5

But before faith came, we were kept under the law, shut up unto the faith which should afterwards be revealed. Wherefore the law was our schoolmaster to bring us unto Christ, that we might be justified by faith. For ye are all the children of God by faith in Christ Jesus.

Galatians 3:23-24 & 26

But the goal of our instruction is love from a pure heart and a good conscience and a sincere faith.

1Timothy 1:5 (NASB)

Even so faith, if it has no works, is dead, being by itself. But are you willing to recognize, you foolish fellow, that faith without works is useless?

James 2:17 & 20 (NASB)

I have fought the good fight, I have finished the course, I have kept the faith;

2 Timothy 4:7 (NASB)

Love

The LORD hath appeared of old unto me, saying, Yea, I have loved thee with an everlasting love: therefore with lovingkindness have I drawn thee.

Jeremiah 31:3

For God so loved the world, that he gave his only begotten Son, that whosoever believeth in him should not perish, but have everlasting life.

John 3:16

But God commendeth his love toward us, in that, while we were yet sinners, Christ died for us.

Romans 5:8

For the Father himself loveth you, because ye have loved me, and have believed that I came out from God.

John 16:27

Behold, what manner of love the Father hath bestowed upon us, that we should be called the sons of God: therefore the world knoweth us not, because it knew him not.

1 John 3:1

But as it is written, Eye hath not seen, nor ear heard, neither have entered into the heart of man, the things which God hath prepared for them that love him.

1 Corinthians 2:9

But if any man love God, the same is known of him.

1 Corinthians 8:3

As the Father hath loved me, so have I loved you: continue ye in my love. If ye keep my commandments, ye shall abide in my love; even as I have kept my Father's commandments, and abide in his love.

John 15:9-10

He that hath my commandments, and keepeth them, he it is that loveth me: and he that loveth me shall be loved of my Father, and I will love him, and will manifest myself to him.

John 14:21

This is my commandment, That ye love one another, as I have loved you. Greater love hath no man than this, that a man lay down his life for his friends. These things I command you, that ye love one another.

John 15:12-13 & 17

A new commandment I give unto you, That ye love one another; as I have loved you, that ye also love one another. By this shall all men know that ye are my disciples, if ye have love one to another.

John 13:34-35

Master, which is the great commandment in the law? Jesus said unto him, Thou shalt love the Lord thy God with all thy heart, and with all thy soul, and with all thy mind. This is the first and great commandment. And the second is like unto it, Thou shalt love thy neighbour as thyself.

Matthew 22:36-39

But I say unto you, love your enemies, bless them that curse you, do good to them that hate you, and pray for them which despitefully use you, and persecute you;

For if ye love them which love you, what reward have ye? do not even the publicans the same?

Matthew 5:44 & 46

And this is love, that we walk after his commandments. This is the commandment, That, as ye have heard from the beginning, ye should walk in it.

2 John 6

Beloved, let us love one another, for love is from God; and everyone who loves is born of God and knows God. The one who does not love does not know God, for God is love. By this the love of God was manifested in us, that God has sent His only begotten Son into the world so that we might live through Him. In this is love, not that we loved God, but that He loved us and sent His Son *to be* the propitiation for our sins. Beloved, if God so loved us, we also ought to love one another. No one has seen God at any time; if we love one another, God abides in us, and His love is perfected in us. By this we know that we abide in Him and He in us, because He has given us of His Spirit. We have seen and testify that the Father has sent the Son *to be* the Savior of the world. Whoever confesses that Jesus is the Son of God, God abides in him, and he in God. We have come to know and have believed the love which God has for us. God is love, and the one who abides in love abides in God, and God abides in him. By this, love is perfected with us, so that we may have confidence in the day of judgment; because as He is, so also are we in this world. There is no fear in love; but perfect love casts out fear, because fear involves punishment, and the one who fears is not perfected in love. We love, because He first loved us. If someone says, "I love God," and hates his brother, he is a liar;

for the one who does not love his brother whom he has seen, cannot love God whom he has not seen.

1 John 4:7-20 (NASB)

If I speak in the tongues of men and of angels, but have not love, I am only a resounding gong, or a clanging cymbal. If I have the gift of prophecy, and can fathom all mysteries, and all knowledge; and if I have a faith that can move mountains, but have not love, I am nothing. If I give all I possess to the poor and surrender my body to the flames, but have not love, I gain nothing. Love is patient, love is kind. It does not envy, it does not boast, it is not proud. It is not rude, it is not self-seeking, it is not easily angered, it keeps no record of wrongs. Love does not delight in evil but rejoices with the truth. It always protects, always trusts, always hopes, always perseveres. Love never fails.

1 Corinthians 13:1-8 (NIV)

And walk in love, as Christ also hath loved us, and hath given himself for us an offering and a sacrifice to God for a sweetsmelling savour.

Ephesians 5:2

And let us consider one another to provoke unto love and to good works.

Hebrews 10:24

For this is the message which you have heard from the beginning, that we should love one another; We know that we have passed out of death into life, because we love the brethren. He who does not love abides in death. Everyone who hates his brother is a murderer; and you know that no murderer has eternal life abiding in him. We know love by this, that He laid

58

down His life for us; and we ought to lay down our lives for the brethren.

1 John 3:11 & 14-16 (NASB)

For God is not unrighteous to forget your work and labour of love, which ye have shewed toward his name, in that ye have ministered to the saints, and do minister.

Hebrews 6:10

Let brotherly love continue.

Hebrews 13:1

For, brethren, ye have been called unto liberty; only use not liberty for an occasion to the flesh, but by love serve one another.

Galatians 5:13

But whoso keepeth his word, in him verily is the love of God perfected: hereby know we that we are in him.

1 John 2:5

And we beseech you, brethren, to know them which labour among you, and are over you in the Lord, and admonish you; And to esteem them very highly in love for their work's sake. And be at peace among yourselves.

Thessalonians 5:12-13

Let love be without dissimulation. Abhor that which is evil; cleave to that which is good. Be kindly affectioned one to another with brotherly love; in honour preferring one another;

Romans 12:9-10

That their hearts might be comforted, being knit together in love, and unto all riches of the full assurance of understanding, to the acknowledgement of the mystery of God, and of the Father, and of Christ; In whom are hid all the treasures of wisdom and knowledge.

Colossians 2:2-3

Owe no man any thing, but to love one another: for he that loveth another hath fulfilled the law. Love worketh no ill to his neighbour: therefore love is the fulfilling of the law.

Romans 13:8 &10

But ye, beloved, building up yourselves on your most holy faith, praying in the Holy Ghost, Keep yourselves in the love of God, looking for the mercy of our Lord Jesus Christ unto eternal life.

Jude 20-21

Above all, love each other deeply, because love covers over a multitude of sins.

1 Peter 4:8 (NIV)

For he that will love life, and see good days, let him refrain his tongue from evil, and his lips that they speak no guile: Let him eschew evil, and do good; let him seek peace, and ensue it.

1 Peter 3:10-11(NIV)

I know your deeds, your love and faith, your service and perseverance, and that you are now doing more than you did at first.

Revelation 2:19 (NIV)

For I am persuaded, that neither death, nor life, nor angels, nor principalities, nor powers, nor things present, nor things to come, Nor height, nor depth, nor any other creature, shall be able to separate us from the love of God, which is in Christ Jesus our Lord.

Romans 8:38-39

...God is love; and he that dwelleth in love dwelleth in God, and God in him.

1 John 4:16

I will sing of the LORD'S great love forever; with my mouth I will make your faithfulness known through all generations. I will declare that your love stands firm forever.

Psalm 89:1-2 (NIV)

The Authority of a Believer

It is very important to know who we are in Christ and the authority that we have in Him. Jesus Christ has already won the victory for us and has given us His Word as an arsenal against the enemy.

Lift up your heads, O ye gates; and be ye lift up, ye everlasting doors; and the King of glory shall come in. Who is this King of glory? The LORD strong and mighty, the LORD mighty in battle. Lift up your heads, O ye gates; even lift them up, ye everlasting doors; and the King of glory shall come in. Who is this King of glory? The LORD of hosts, he is the King of glory. Selah.

Psalm 24:7-10

Through God we shall do valiantly: for he it is that shall tread down our enemies.

Psalm 108:13

Then he answered and spake unto me, saying, This is the word of the LORD...Not by might, nor power, but by my spirit, saith the LORD of hosts.

Zechariah 4:6

This I say then, Walk in the Spirit, and ye shall not fulfill the lust of the flesh. For the flesh lusteth against the Spirit, and the Spirit against the flesh: and these are contrary the one to the other: so that ye cannot do the things that ye would.

Galatians 5:16-17

Jesus said unto him, If thou canst believe, all things are possible to him that believeth.

Mark 9:23

For though we walk in the flesh, we do not war after the flesh: (For the weapons of our warfare are not carnal, but mighty through God to the pulling down of strongholds;) Casting down imaginations, and every high thing that exalteth itself against the knowledge of God, and bringing into captivity every thought to the obedience of Christ;

2 Corinthians 10:3-5

Submit yourselves therefore to God. Resist the devil, and he will flee from you. Draw nigh to God, and he will draw nigh to you. Cleanse your hands, ye sinners; and purify your hearts, ye double minded.

James 4:7-8

Behold, I give unto you power to tread on serpents and scorpions, and over all the power of the enemy: and nothing shall by any means hurt you.

Luke 10:19

And I will give unto thee the keys of the kingdom of heaven: and whatsoever thou shalt bind on earth shall be bound in heaven: and whatsoever thou shalt loose on earth shall be loosed in heaven.

Matthew 16:19

No weapon that is formed against thee shall prosper; and every tongue that shall rise against thee in judgment thou shalt condemn. This is the heritage of the servants of the LORD, and their righteousness is of me, saith the LORD.

Isaiah 54:17

Be sober, be vigilant; because your adversary the devil, as a roaring lion, walketh about, seeking whom he may devour:

1 Peter 5:8

What shall we then say to these things? If God be for us, who can be against us?

Romans 8:31

Verily I say unto you, Whatsoever ye shall bind on earth shall be bound in heaven: and whatsoever ye shall loose on earth shall be loosed in heaven.

Matthew 18:18

And let us not be weary in well doing: for in due season we shall reap, if we faint not.

Galatians 6:9

To him that overcometh will I grant to sit with me in my throne, even as I also overcame, and am set down with my Father in his throne.

Revelation 3:21

For the eyes of the LORD run to and fro throughout the whole earth, to shew himself strong in the behalf of them whose heart is perfect toward him.

2 Chronicles 16:9

Finally, my brethren, be strong in the Lord, and in the power of his might. Put on the whole armour of God, that ye may be able to stand against the wiles of the devil. For we wrestle not against flesh and blood, but against principalities, against powers, against the rulers of the darkness of this world, against spiritual wickedness in high places. Wherefore take unto you the whole armour of God, that ye may be able to withstand in the evil day, and having done all, to stand.

Stand therefore, having your loins girt about with truth, and having on the breastplate of righteousness; And your feet shod with the preparation of the gospel of peace; Above all, taking the shield of faith, wherewith ye shall be able to quench all the fiery darts of the wicked. And take the helmet of salvation, and the sword of the Spirit, which is the word of God: Praying always with all prayer and supplication in the Spirit, and watching thereunto with all perseverance and supplication for all saints;

Ephesians 6:10-18

But the men marveled, saying, What manner of man is this, that even the winds and the sea obey him!

Matthew 8:27

And Jesus came and spake unto them, saying, All power is given unto me in heaven and in earth. Go ye therefore, and teach all nations, baptizing them in the name of the Father, and of the Son, and of the Holy Ghost: Teaching them to observe all things whatsoever I have commanded you: and, lo, I am with you always, even unto the end of the world. Amen.

Matthew 28:18-20

GOD'S WORD FOR DAILY LIVING

Personal Devotion

Spending time with our Heavenly Father and meditating on His Word helps us to develop a close relationship with Him. The God of the universe wants to have a close relationship with His Creation. The more we spend time with Him, and in His Word, the closer we will get to Him.

This is the day which the LORD hath made; we will rejoice and be glad in it.

Psalm 118:24

O God, thou art my God; early will I seek thee: my soul thirsteth for thee, my flesh longeth for thee in a dry and thirsty land, where no water is; To see thy power and thy glory, so as I have seen thee in the sanctuary. Because thy lovingkindness is better than life, my lips shall praise thee. Thus will I bless thee while I live: I will lift up my hands in thy name. My soul shall be satisfied as with marrow and fatness; and my mouth shall praise thee with joyful lips: When I remember thee upon my bed, and meditate on thee in the night watches. Because thou hast been my help, therefore in the shadow of thy wings will I rejoice.

Psalm 63:1-7

Cause me to hear thy lovingkindness in the morning; for in thee do I trust: cause me to know the way wherein I should walk; for I lift up my soul unto thee.

Psalm 143:8

When thou saidst, Seek ye my face; my heart said unto thee, Thy face, LORD, will I seek.

Psalm 27:8

Thou hast proved mine heart; thou hast visited me in the night; thou hast tried me, and shalt find nothing; I am purposed that my mouth shall not transgress.

Psalm 17:3

Search me, O God, and know my heart: try me, and know my thoughts:

Psalm 139:23

I said, I will take heed to my ways, that I sin not with my tongue: I will keep my mouth with a bridle, while the wicked is before me.

Psalm 39:1

I will sing of mercy and judgment: unto thee, O LORD, will I sing. I will behave myself wisely in a perfect way. O when wilt thou come unto me? I will walk within my house with a perfect heart. I will set no wicked thing before mine eyes: I hate the work of them that turn aside; it shall not cleave to me.

Psalm 101:1-3

I the LORD search the heart, I try the reins, even to give every man according to his ways, and according to the fruit of his doings.

Jeremiah 17:10

Thou art my God, and I will praise thee: thou art my God, I will exalt thee. O give thanks unto the LORD; for he is good: for his mercy endureth for ever.

Psalm 118:28-29

Set a watch, O LORD, before my mouth; keep the door of my lips.

Psalm 141:3

Create in me a clean heart, O God; and renew a right spirit within me. Cast me not away from thy presence; and take not thy holy spirit from me. Restore unto me the joy of thy salvation; and uphold me with thy free spirit. Then will I teach transgressors thy ways; and sinners shall be converted unto thee. Deliver me from bloodguiltiness, O God, thou God of my salvation: and my tongue shall sing aloud of thy righteousness. O Lord, open thou my lips; and my mouth shall shew forth thy praise. For thou desirest not sacrifice; else would I give it: thou delightest not in burnt offering. The sacrifices of God are a broken spirit: a broken and a contrite heart, O God, thou wilt not despise. Do good in thy good pleasure unto Zion: build thou the walls of Jerusalem. Then shalt thou be pleased with the sacrifices of righteousness, with burnt offering and whole burnt offering: then shall they offer bullocks upon thine altar.

Psalm 51:10-19

Bless the LORD, O my soul: and all that is within me, bless his holy name. Bless the LORD, O my soul, and forget not all his benefits: Who forgiveth all thine iniquities; who healeth all thy diseases; Who redeemeth thy life from destruction; who crowneth thee with lovingkindness and tender mercies;

Who satisfieth thy mouth with good things; so that thy youth is renewed like the eagle's. The LORD executeth righteousness and judgment for all that are oppressed. He made known his ways unto Moses, his acts unto the children of Israel. The LORD is merciful and gracious, slow to anger, and plenteous in mercy. He will not always chide: neither will he keep his anger for ever. He hath not dealt with us after our sins; nor rewarded us according to our iniquities. For as the heaven is high above the earth, so great is his mercy toward them that fear him. As far as the east is from the west, so far hath he removed our transgressions from us. Like as a father pitieth his children, so the LORD pitieth them that fear him. For he knoweth our frame; he remembereth that we are dust. As for man, his days are as grass: as a flower of the field, so he flourisheth. For the wind passeth over it, and it is gone; and the place thereof shall know it no more. But the mercy of the LORD is from everlasting to everlasting upon them that fear him, and his righteousness unto children's children; To such as keep his covenant, and to those that remember his commandments to do them. The LORD hath prepared his throne in the heavens; and his kingdom ruleth over all. Bless the LORD, ye his angels, that excel in strength, that do his commandments, hearkening unto the voice of his word. Bless ye the LORD, all ye his hosts; ye ministers of his, that do his pleasure. Bless the LORD, all his works in all places of his dominion: bless the LORD, O my soul.

Psalm 103:1-22

Finally, brethren, whatsoever things are true, whatsoever things are honest, whatsoever things are just, whatsoever things are pure, whatsoever things are lovely, whatsoever things are of good report; if there be any virtue, and if there be any praise, think on these things.

Philippians 4:8

I thought on my ways, and turned my feet unto thy testimonies. I made haste, and delayed not to keep thy commandments. The bands of the wicked have robbed me: but I have not forgotten thy law. At midnight I will rise to give thanks unto thee because of thy righteous judgments. I am a companion of all them that fear thee, and of them that keep thy precepts. The earth, O LORD, is full of thy mercy: teach me thy statutes. Thou hast dealt well with thy servant, O LORD, according unto thy word. Teach me good judgment and knowledge: for I have believed thy commandments.

Psalm 119:59-66

Open thou mine eyes, that I may behold wondrous things out of thy law. I am a stranger in the earth: hide not thy commandments from me. My soul breaketh for the longing that it hath unto thy judgments at all times.

Psalm 119:18-20

Teach me, O LORD, the way of thy statutes; and I shall keep it unto the end. Give me understanding, and I shall keep thy law; yea, I shall observe it with my whole heart. Make me to go in the path of thy commandments; for therein do I delight.

Psalm 119:33-35

O LORD our Lord, how excellent is thy name in all the earth! who hast set thy glory above the heavens. Out of the mouth of babes and sucklings hast thou ordained strength because of thine enemies, that thou mightest still the enemy and the avenger. When I consider thy heavens, the work of thy fingers, the moon and the stars, which thou hast ordained; What is man, that thou art mindful of him? and the son of man, that thou visitest him? For thou hast made him a little lower than the angels, and hast crowned him with glory and honour. Thou madest him to have dominion over the works of thy hands; thou hast put all things under his feet: All sheep and oxen, yea, and the beasts of the field; The fowl of the air, and the fish of the sea, and whatsoever passeth through the paths of the seas. O LORD our Lord, how excellent is thy name in all the earth!

Psalm 8:1-9

And take not the word of truth utterly out of my mouth; for I have hoped in thy judgments. So shall I keep thy law continually for ever and ever. And I will walk at liberty: for I seek thy precepts. I will speak of thy testimonies also before kings, and will not be ashamed. And I will delight myself in thy commandments, which I have loved. My hands also will I lift up unto thy commandments, which I have loved; and I will meditate in thy statutes.

Psalm 119:43-48

Thy testimonies have I taken as an heritage for ever: for they are the rejoicing of my heart.

Psalm 119:111

O how love I thy law! it is my meditation all the day. Thou through thy commandments hast made me wiser than mine enemies: for they are ever with me. I have more understanding than all my teachers: for thy testimonies are my meditation. I understand more than the ancients, because I keep thy precepts.

Psalm 119:97-100

The Overcoming Power of Thanksgiving and Praise

An invaluable part of the Christian life is in the realm of giving praise and thanks to God. Praise and thanksgiving bring us into the presence of God; in fact, God inhabits the praises of His people.

Enter into his gates with thanksgiving, and into his courts with praise: be thankful unto him, and bless his name.

Psalm 100:4

O give thanks unto the LORD, for he is good: for his mercy endureth for ever. Oh that men would praise the LORD for his goodness, and for his wonderful works to the children of men! For he satisfieth the longing soul, and filleth the hungry soul with goodness.

Psalm 107:1 & 8-9

Let the high praises of God be in their mouth, and a two-edged sword in their hand;

Psalm 149:6

Praise ye the LORD. O give thanks unto the LORD; for he is good: for his mercy endureth for ever. Who can utter the mighty acts of the LORD? who can shew forth all his praise?

Psalm 106:1-2

While I live will I praise the LORD: I will sing praises unto my God while I have any being.

Psalm 146:2

Let them praise the name of the LORD: for his name alone is excellent; his glory is above the earth and heaven.

Psalm 148:13

I will sing of the mercies of the LORD for ever: with my mouth will I make known thy faithfulness to all generations.

Psalm 89:1

Praise ye the LORD: for it is good to sing praises unto our God; for it is pleasant; and praise is comely.

Psalm 147:1

O come, let us sing unto the LORD: let us make a joyful noise to the rock of our salvation.

Psalm 95:1

My lips shall greatly rejoice when I sing unto thee; and my soul, which thou hast redeemed.

Psalm 71:23

Sing unto God, ye kingdoms of the earth; O sing praises unto the Lord; Selah:

Psalm 68:32

Sing unto God, sing praises to his name: extol him that rideth upon the heavens by his name JAH, and rejoice before him. .

Psalm 68:4

Praise the LORD; for the LORD is good: sing praises unto his name; for it is pleasant.

Psalm 135:2-3

O give thanks unto the LORD; for he is good: because his mercy endureth for ever.

Psalm 118:1

Then shalt thou delight thyself in the LORD; and I will cause thee to ride upon the high places of the earth, and feed thee with the heritage of Jacob thy father: for the mouth of the LORD hath spoken it.

Isaiah 58:14

By him therefore let us offer the sacrifice of praise to God continually, that is, the fruit of our lips giving thanks to his name.

Hebrews 13:15

So will I sing praise unto thy name for ever, that I may daily perform my vows.

Psalm 61:8

The pastures are clothed with flocks; the valleys also are covered over with corn; they shout for joy, they also sing.

Psalm 65:13

O let the nations be glad and sing for joy: for thou shalt judge the people righteously, and govern the nations upon earth. Selah.

Psalm 67:4

Praise ye the LORD. Sing unto the LORD a new song, and his praise in the congregation of saints.

Psalm 149:1

Praise ye the LORD. Praise, O ye servants of the LORD praise the name of the LORD.

Psalm 113:1

I will bless the LORD at all times: his praise shall continually be in my mouth. My soul shall make her boast in the LORD: the humble shall hear thereof, and be glad. O magnify the LORD with me, and let us exalt his name together. I sought the LORD, and he heard me, and delivered me from all my fears. They looked unto him, and were lightened: and their faces were not ashamed. This poor man cried, and the LORD heard him, and saved him out of all his troubles. The angel of the LORD encampeth round about them that fear him, and delivereth them. O taste and see that the LORD is good: blessed is the man that trusteth in him. O fear the LORD, ye his saints: for there is no want to them that fear him. The young lions do lack, and suffer hunger: but they that seek the LORD shall not want any good thing. Come, ye children, hearken unto me: I will teach you the fear of the LORD. What man is he that desireth life, and loveth many days, that he may see good? Keep thy tongue from evil, and thy lips from speaking guile. Depart from evil, and do good; seek peace, and pursue it. The eyes of the LORD are upon the righteous, and his ears are open unto their cry. The face of the LORD is against them that do evil, to cut off the remembrance of them from the earth. The righteous cry, and the LORD heareth, and delivereth them out of all their troubles. The LORD is nigh unto them that are of a broken heart; and saveth such as be of a contrite spirit. Many are the afflictions of the righteous: but the LORD delivereth him out of them all. He keepeth all his bones: not one of them is broken. Evil shall slay the wicked: and they that hate the righteous shall be desolate. The LORD redeemeth the soul of his servants: and none of them that trust in him shall be desolate.

Psalm 34:1-22

I will exalt you, my God the King; I will praise your
name for ever and ever. Every day I will praise you
and extol your name for ever and ever. Great is the
LORD and most worthy of praise; his greatness no
one can fathom. One generation will commend your
works to another; they will tell of your mighty acts.
They will speak of the glorious splendor of your
majesty, and I will meditate on your wonderful
works. They will tell of the power of your awesome
works, and I will proclaim your great deeds. They
will celebrate your abundant goodness and joyfully
sing of your righteousness. The LORD is gracious
and compassionate, slow to anger and rich in love.
The LORD is good to all; he has compassion on all
he has made. All you have made will praise you, O
LORD; your saints will extol you. They will tell of
the glory of your kingdom and speak of your might,
so that all men may know of your mighty acts and the
glorious splendor of your kingdom. Your kingdom is
an everlasting kingdom, and your dominion endures
through all generations. The LORD is faithful to all
his promises and loving toward all he has made. The
LORD upholds all those who fall and lifts up all who
are bowed down. The eyes of all look to you, and you
give them their food at the proper time. You open your
hand and satisfy the desires of every living thing. The
LORD is righteous in all his ways and loving toward
all he has made. The LORD is near to all who call
on him, to all who call on him in truth. He fulfills the
desires of those who fear him; he hears their cry and
saves them. The LORD watches over all who love
him, but all the wicked he will destroy. My mouth
will speak in praise of the LORD. Let every creature
praise his holy name for ever and ever.

Psalm 145:1-21 (NIV)

I will praise thee with my whole heart: before the gods will I sing praise unto thee. I will worship toward thy holy temple, and praise thy name for thy lovingkindness and for thy truth: for thou hast magnified thy word above all thy name.

Psalm 138:1- 2

Praise ye the LORD. I will praise the LORD with my whole heart, in the assembly of the upright, and in the congregation.

Psalm 111:1

In God we boast all the day long, and praise thy name for ever. Selah.

Psalm 44:8

Exalt the LORD our God, and worship at his holy hill; for the LORD our God is holy.

Psalm 99:9

This people have I formed for myself; they shall shew forth my praise.

Isaiah 43:21

Praise ye the LORD. Praise God in his sanctuary: praise him in the firmament of his power. Praise him for his mighty acts: praise him according to his excellent greatness. Praise him with the sound of the trumpet: praise him with the psaltery and harp. Praise him with the timbrel and dance: praise him with stringed instruments and organs. Praise him upon the loud cymbals: praise him upon the high sounding cymbals. Let every thing that hath breath praise the LORD. Praise ye the LORD.

Psalm 150:1-6

O LORD my God, you are very great; you are clothed with splendor and majesty. He wraps himself in light as with a garment; he stretches out the heavens like a tent and lays the beams of his upper chambers on their waters. He makes the clouds his chariot and rides on the wings of the wind. He makes winds his messengers, flames of fire his servants. He set the earth on its foundations; it can never be moved. You covered it with the deep as with a garment; the waters stood above the mountains. But at your rebuke the waters fled, at the sound of your thunder they took to flight; they flowed over the mountains, they went down into the valleys, to the place you assigned for them. You set a boundary they cannot cross; never again will they cover the earth. He makes springs pour water into the ravines; it flows between the mountains. They give water to all the beasts of the field; the wild donkeys quench their thirst. The birds of the air nest by the waters; they sing among the branches. He waters the mountains from his upper chambers; the earth is satisfied by the fruit of his work. He makes grass grow for the cattle, and plants for man to cultivate—bringing forth food from the earth: The trees of the LORD are well watered, the cedars of Lebanon that he planted. There the birds make their nests; the stork has its home in the pine trees. The high mountains belong to the wild goats; the crags are a refuge for the coneys. The moon marks off the seasons, and the sun knows when to go down. You bring darkness, it becomes night, and all the beasts of the forest prowl. The lions roar for their prey and seek their food from God. The sun rises, and they steal away; they return and lie down in their dens. Then man goes out to his work, to his labor until evening. How many are your works, O LORD! In wisdom you made them all; the earth is full of your creatures. There is the sea, vast and spacious, teeming with creatures beyond number—living things both large and small. There the ships go to and fro, and the leviathan, which you formed to frolic there. These all look to you to give them their food at the proper time. When you give it to them, they gather it up; when you open your hand, they are satisfied with good things. When you hide your face, they are terrified; when you take away their breath, they die and return to the dust. When you send your Spirit, they are created, and you renew the face of the earth. May the glory of the LORD endure forever; may the LORD rejoice in his works—he who looks at the earth, and it trembles, who touches the mountains, and they smoke. I will sing to the LORD all my life; I will sing praise to my God as long as I live. May my meditation be pleasing to him, as I rejoice in the LORD.

Psalm 104:1-14 & 16-34 (NIV)

It is a good thing to give thanks unto the LORD, and to sing praises unto thy name, O most High:

Psalm 92:1

O sing unto the LORD a new song: sing unto the LORD, all the earth. Sing unto the LORD, bless his name; shew forth his salvation from day to day. Declare his glory among the heathen, his wonders among all people. For the LORD is great, and greatly to be praised: he is to be feared above all gods. For all the gods of the nations are idols: but the LORD made the heavens. Honour and majesty are before him: strength and beauty are in his sanctuary. Give unto the LORD, O ye kindreds of the people, give unto the LORD glory and strength. Give unto the

LORD the glory due unto his name: bring an offering, and come into his courts. O worship the LORD in the beauty of holiness: fear before him, all the earth. Say among the heathen that the LORD reigneth: the world also shall be established that it shall not be moved: he shall judge the people righteously. Let the heavens rejoice, and let the earth be glad; let the sea roar, and the fullness thereof. Let the field be joyful, and all that is therein: then shall all the trees of the wood rejoice Before the LORD: for he cometh, for he cometh to judge the earth: he shall judge the world with righteousness, and the people with his truth.

Psalm 96:1-13

O sing unto the LORD a new song; for he hath done marvelous things: his right hand, and his holy arm, hath gotten him the victory. The LORD hath made known his salvation: his righteousness hath he openly shewed in the sight of the heathen. He hath remembered his mercy and his truth toward the house of Israel: all the ends of the earth have seen the salvation of our God. Make a joyful noise unto the LORD, all the earth: make a loud noise, and rejoice, and sing praise. Sing unto the LORD with the harp; with the harp, and the voice of a psalm. With trumpets and sound of cornet make a joyful noise before the LORD, the King. Let the sea roar, and the fullness thereof; the world, and they that dwell therein. Let the floods clap their hands: let the hills be joyful together

Psalm 98:1-8

The LORD reigneth; let the earth rejoice; let the multitude of isles be glad thereof. Clouds and darkness are round about him: righteousness and judgment are the habitation of his throne. A fire goeth before him, and burneth up his enemies round about. His lightnings enlightened the world: the earth saw, and trembled. The hills melted like wax at the presence of the LORD, at the presence of the Lord of the whole earth. The heavens declare his righteousness, and all the people see his glory. Confounded be all they that serve graven images, that boast themselves of idols: worship him, all ye gods. Zion heard, and was glad; and the daughters of Judah rejoiced because of thy judgments, O LORD. For thou, LORD, art high above all the earth: thou art exalted far above all gods. Ye that love the LORD, hate evil: he preserveth the souls of his saints; he delivereth them out of the hand of the wicked. Light is sown for the righteous, and gladness for the upright in heart. Rejoice in the LORD, ye righteous; and give thanks at the remembrance of his holiness.

Psalm 97:1-12

Be thou exalted, LORD, in thine own strength: so will we sing and praise thy power.

Psalm 21:13

Praise ye the Lord, all ye nations: praise Him, all ye people.

Psalm 117:1

O give thanks unto the LORD; call upon his name: make known his deeds among the people. Sing unto him, sing psalms unto him: talk ye of all his wondrous works. Glory ye in his holy name: let the heart of them rejoice that seek the LORD. Seek the LORD, and his strength: seek his face evermore. Remember his marvelous works that he hath done; his wonders, and the judgments of his mouth;

Psalm 105:1-5

Thou art worthy, O Lord, to receive glory and honour and power: for thou hast created all things, and for thy pleasure they are and were created.

Revelation 4:11

And I beheld, and I heard the voice of many angels round about the throne and the beasts and the elders: and the number of them was ten thousand times ten thousand, and thousands of thousands; Saying with a loud voice, Worthy is the Lamb that was slain to receive power, and riches, and wisdom, and strength, and honour, and glory, and blessing. And every creature which is in heaven, and on the earth, and under the earth, and such as are in the sea, and all that are in them, heard I saying, Blessing, and honour, and glory, and power, be unto him that sitteth upon the throne, and unto the Lamb for ever and ever.

Revelation 5:11-13

Worship

God made us to worship Him. Worshipping God takes us into His glory.

O come, let us worship and bow down: let us kneel before the LORD our maker.

Psalm 95:6

Give unto the LORD the glory due unto his name: bring an offering, and come before him: worship the LORD in the beauty of holiness.

1 Chronicles 16:29

But as for me, I will come into thy house in the multitude of thy mercy: and in thy fear will I worship toward thy holy temple.

Psalm 5:7

We will go into his tabernacles: we will worship at his footstool. Arise, O LORD, into thy rest; thou, and the ark of thy strength. Let thy priests be clothed with righteousness; and let thy saints shout for joy.

Psalm 132:7-9

Exalt ye the LORD our God, and worship at his footstool; for he is holy. Moses and Aaron among his priests, and Samuel among them that call upon his name; they called upon the LORD, and he answered them. He spake unto them in the cloudy pillar: they kept his testimonies, and the ordinance that he gave them. Thou answeredst them, O LORD our God: thou wast a God that forgavest them, though thou tookest vengeance of their inventions. Exalt the LORD our God, and worship at his holy hill; for the LORD our

God is holy.

Psalm 99:5-9

All the ends of the world shall remember and turn unto the LORD: and all the kindreds of the nations shall worship before thee.

Psalm 22:27

So shall the king greatly desire thy beauty: for he is thy Lord; and worship thou him.

Psalm 45:11

And it shall come to pass, that from one new moon to another, and from one Sabbath to another, shall all flesh come to worship before me, saith the LORD.

Isaiah 66:23

The LORD will be terrible unto them: for he will famish all the gods of the earth; and men shall worship him, every one from his place, even all the isles of the heathen.

Zephaniah 2:11

There shall no strange god be in thee; neither shalt thou worship any strange god. I am the LORD thy God, which brought thee out of the land of Egypt: open thy mouth wide, and I will fill it.

Psalm 81:9-10

All the earth shall worship thee, and shall sing unto thee; they shall sing to thy name. Selah.

Psalm 66:4

I will worship toward thy holy temple, and praise thy name for thy lovingkindness and for thy truth: for thou hast magnified thy word above all thy name.

Psalm 138:2

For we are the circumcision, which worship God in the spirit, and rejoice in Christ Jesus, and have no confidence in the flesh.

Philippians 3:3

And again, when He bringeth in the First Begotten into the world, He saith, And let all the angels of God worship Him.

Hebrews 1:6

All the earth shall worship thee, and shall sing unto thee; they shall sing to thy name. Selah.

Psalm 66:4

Give unto the LORD the glory due unto His name; worship the LORD in the beauty of holiness.

Psalm 29:2

Then Nebuchadnezzar spake, and said, Blessed be the God of Shadrach, Meshach, and Abednego, who hath sent his angel, and delivered his servants that trusted in him, and have changed the king's word, and yielded their bodies, that they might not serve nor worship any god, except their own God. Therefore I make a decree, That every people, nation, and language, which speak any thing amiss against the God of Shadrach, Meshach, and Abednego, shall be cut in pieces, and their houses shall be made a dunghill: because there is no other God that can deliver after this sort. Then the king promoted Shadrach, Meshach, and Abednego, in the province of Babylon.

Daniel 3:28-30

Our fathers worshiped in this mountain, and you people say that in Jerusalem is the place where men ought to worship." Jesus said to her, "Woman, believe Me, an hour is coming when neither in this mountain nor in Jerusalem will you worship the Father. You worship what you do not know; we worship what we know, for salvation is from the Jews. But an hour is coming, and now is, when the true worshipers will worship the Father in spirit and truth; for such people the Father seeks to be His worshipers. God is spirit, and those who worship Him must worship in spirit and truth." The woman said to Him, "I know that Messiah is coming (He who is called Christ); when that One comes, He will declare all things to us." Jesus said to her, "I who speak to you am He."

John 4:20-26 (NASB)

And I John saw these things, and heard them. And when I had heard and seen, I fell down to worship before the feet of the angel which shewed me these things. Then saith he unto me, See thou do it not: for I am thy fellowservant, and of thy brethren the prophets, and of them which keep the sayings of this book: worship God.

Revelation 22:8-9

Prayer

The Son of God, our Lord Jesus Christ, was a man of prayer. Prayer is communion with our Heavenly Father. It is the key that unlocks the miracles of God's treasures.

And in the morning, rising up a great while before day, he went out, and departed into a solitary place, and there prayed.

Mark 1:35

And it came to pass in those days, that he went out into a mountain to pray, and continued all night in prayer to God.

Luke 6:12

And he was withdrawn from them about a stone's cast, and kneeled down, and prayed,

Luke 22:41

And it came to pass, that, as he was praying in a certain place, when he ceased, one of his disciples said unto him, Lord, teach us to pray, as John also taught his disciples.

Luke 11:1

And I say unto you, Ask, and it shall be given you; seek, and ye shall find; knock, and it shall be opened unto you.

Luke 11:9

During the days of Jesus' life on earth, he offered up prayers and petitions with loud cries and tears to the one who could save him from death, and he was heard because of his reverent submission.

Hebrews 5:7 (NIV)

Someone said, "Pray like it's all up to God and work like it's all up to you!"

God wants to answer our prayer. In order to get our prayer answered, we need to know how to pray.

1. Pray to God in the name of Jesus.
And whatsoever ye shall ask in my name, that will I do, that the Father may be glorified in the Son. If ye shall ask any thing in my name, I will do it.

John 14:13-14

Truly, truly, I say to you, if you ask the Father for anything in My name, He will give it to you. Until now you have asked for nothing in My name; ask and you will receive, so that your joy may be made full.

John 16:23-24 (NASB)

Giving thanks always for all things unto God and the Father in the name of our Lord Jesus Christ;

Ephesians 5:20

2. Stand firm on God's promises, because He will bring it to pass all He has promised us.
God is not a man, that he should lie, nor a son of man, that he should change his mind. Does he speak and then not act? Does he promise and not fulfill?

Numbers 23:19 (NIV)

Blessed be the LORD, that hath given rest unto his people Israel, according to all that he promised: there hath not failed one word of all his good promise, which he promised by the hand of Moses his servant.

1 Kings 8:56

...The LORD is faithful to all his promises and loving toward all he has made.

Psalm 145:13 (NIV)

3. We must not to let doubt and unbelief control our emotions.

Be careful for nothing; but in everything by prayer and supplication with thanksgiving let your requests be made known unto God. And the peace of God, which passeth all understanding, shall keep your hearts and minds through Christ Jesus.

Philippians 4:6-7

Casting down imaginations, and every high thing that exalteth itself against the knowledge of God, and bringing into captivity every thought to the obedience of Christ;

2 Corinthians 10:5

4. Look beyond the situation and continue standing on the promises of God and declaring God's full and timely provision.

He staggered not at the promise of God through unbelief; but was strong in faith, giving glory to God;

Romans 4:20

Now faith is the substance of things hoped for, the evidence of things not seen.

Hebrews 11:1

5. Pray the word of God because He honors His word.

The LORD said to me, You have seen correctly, for I

am watching to see that my word is fulfilled.

Jeremiah 1:12 (NIV)

So shall my word be that goeth forth out of my mouth: it shall not return unto me void, but it shall accomplish that which I please, and it shall prosper in the thing whereto I sent it.

Isaiah 55:11

6. Pray, because it works!

...The effectual fervent prayer of a righteous man availeth much.

James 5:16

More on Prayer

If ye abide in me, and my words abide in you, ye shall ask what ye will, and it shall be done unto you.

John 15:7

Verily, verily, I say unto you, He that believeth on me, the works that I do shall he do also; and greater works than these shall he do; because I go unto my Father.

John 14:12

Jesus saith unto her, Said I not unto thee, that, if thou wouldest believe, thou shouldest see the glory of God?

John 11:40

For verily I say unto you, That whosoever shall say unto this mountain, Be thou removed, and be thou cast into the sea; and shall not doubt in his heart, but shall believe that those things which he saith shall come to pass; he shall have whatsoever he saith. Therefore I say unto you, What things soever ye desire, when ye pray, believe that ye receive them, and ye shall have them. And when ye stand praying, forgive, if ye have ought against any: that your Father also which is in heaven may forgive you your trespasses. But if ye do not forgive, neither will your Father which is in heaven forgive your trespasses.

Mark 11:23-26

And he said unto them, This kind can come forth by nothing, but by prayer and fasting.

Mark 9:29

If any of you lack wisdom, let him ask of God, that giveth to all men liberally, and upbraideth not; and it shall be given him.

James 1:5

For I know the thoughts that I think toward you, saith the LORD, thoughts of peace, and not of evil, to give you an expected end. Then shall ye call upon me, and ye shall go and pray unto me, and I will hearken unto you.

Jeremiah 29:11-12

And this is the confidence that we have in him, that, if we ask any thing according to his will, he heareth us: And if we know that he hear us, whatsoever we ask, we know that we have the petitions that we desired of him.

1 John 5:14-15

Ye have not chosen me, but I have chosen you, and ordained you, that ye should go and bring forth fruit, and that your fruit should remain: that whatsoever ye shall ask of the Father in my name, he may give it you.

John 15:16

So Peter was kept in the prison, but prayer for him was being made fervently by the church to God. On the very night when Herod was about to bring him forward, Peter was sleeping between two soldiers, bound with two chains, and guards in front of the door were watching over the prison. And behold, an angel of the Lord suddenly appeared and a light shone in the cell; and he struck Peter's side and woke him up, saying, "Get up quickly." And his chains fell off his hands. And the angel said to him, "Gird yourself and put on your sandals." And he did so. And he said to him, "Wrap your cloak around you and follow me." And he went out and continued to follow, and he did not know that what was being done by the angel was real, but thought he was seeing a vision. When they had passed the first and second guard, they came to the iron gate that leads into the city, which opened for them by itself; and they went out and went along one street, and immediately the angel departed from him. When Peter came to himself, he said, "Now I know for sure that the Lord has sent forth His angel and rescued me from the hand of Herod and from all that the Jewish people were expecting."

Acts 12:5-11 (NASB)

Elias was a man subject to like passions as we are, and he prayed earnestly that it might not rain: and it rained not on the earth by the space of three years and six months. And he prayed again, and the heaven gave rain, and the earth brought forth her fruit.

James 5:17-18

And when they had prayed, the place was shaken where they were assembled together; and they were all filled with the Holy Ghost, and they spake the word of God with boldness.

Acts 4:31

Praying always with all prayer and supplication in the Spirit, and watching thereunto with all perseverance and supplication for all saints.

Ephesians 6:18

Likewise the Spirit also helpeth our infirmities: for we know not what we should pray for as we ought: but the Spirit itself maketh intercession for us with groanings which cannot be uttered. And he that searcheth the hearts knoweth what is the mind of the Spirit, because he maketh intercession for the saints according to the will of God.

Romans 8:26-27

And God is able to make all grace abound toward you; that ye, always having all sufficiency in all things, may abound to every good work:

2 Corinthians 9:8

Watch and pray, that ye enter not into temptation: the spirit indeed is willing, but the flesh is weak.

Matthew 26:41

Beloved, if our heart condemn us not, then have we confidence toward God. And whatsoever we ask, we receive of him, because we keep his commandments, and do those things that are pleasing in his sight.

1 John 3:21-23

Remember me, O LORD, with the favour that thou bearest unto thy people: O visit me with thy salvation;

Psalm 106:4

O thou that hearest prayer, unto thee shall all flesh come.

Psalm 65:2

Delight thyself also in the LORD; and he shall give thee the desires of thine heart.

Psalm 37:4

My soul, wait thou only upon God; for my expectation is from him. He only is my rock and my salvation: he is my defense; I shall not be moved.

Psalm 62:5-6

I love the LORD, because he hath heard my voice and my supplications. Because he hath inclined his ear unto me, therefore will I call upon him as long as I live.

Psalm 116:1-4

In the day when I cried thou answeredst me, and strengthenedst me with strength in my soul.

Psalm 138:3

I will praise thee: for thou hast heard me, and art become my salvation. This is the LORD'S doing; it is marvellous in our eyes.

Psalm 118:21 & 23

And I sought for a man among them, that should make up the hedge, and stand in the gap before me for the land, that I should not destroy it: but I found none.

Ezekiel 22:30

...He is a rewarder of them that diligently seek him

Hebrew 11:6

...ye have not, because ye ask not.

James 4:2

And he spake a parable unto them to this end, that men ought always to pray, and not to faint;

Luke 18:1

Pray without ceasing.

1 Thessalonians 5:17

Fear Not

Fear is not from God. Fear makes you feel helpless. But you can overcome fear by meditating on God's Word and by seeking Him. Fear brings defeat, but faith in God brings hope and deliverance.

Fear not: for I have redeemed thee, I have called thee by thy name; thou art mine. When thou passest through the waters, I will be with thee; and through the rivers, they shall not overflow thee: when thou walkest through the fire, thou shalt not be burned; neither shall the flame kindle upon thee. For I am the LORD thy God, the Holy One of Israel, thy Saviour:

Isaiah 43:1-3

Be strong and of a good courage, fear not, nor be afraid of them: for the LORD thy God, he it is that doth go with thee; he will not fail thee, nor forsake thee. And the LORD, he it is that doth go before thee; he will be with thee, he will not fail thee, neither forsake thee: fear not, neither be dismayed.

Deuteronomy 31:6 & 8

Come unto me, all ye that labour and are heavy laden, and I will give you rest. Take my yoke upon you, and learn of me; for I am meek and lowly in heart: and ye shall find rest unto your souls. For my yoke is easy, and my burden is light.

Matthew 11:28-30

Fear not, little flock; for it is your Father's good pleasure to give you the kingdom.

Luke 12:32

Fear thou not; for I am with thee: be not dismayed; for I am thy God: I will strengthen thee; yea, I will help thee; yea, I will uphold thee with the right hand of my righteousness.

Isaiah 41:10

"Therefore I tell you, do not worry about your life, what you will eat or drink; or about your body, what you will wear. Is not life more important than food, and the body more important than clothes? Look at the birds of the air; they do not sow or reap or store away in barns, and yet your heavenly Father feeds them. Are you not much more valuable than they? Who of you by worrying can add a single hour to his life? "And why do you worry about clothes? See how the lilies of the field grow. They do not labor or spin. Yet I tell you that not even Solomon in all his splendor was dressed like one of these. If that is how God clothes the grass of the field, which is here today and tomorrow is thrown into the fire, will he not much more clothe you, O you of little faith? So do not worry, saying, 'What shall we eat?' or 'What shall we drink?' or 'What shall we wear?' For the pagans run after all these things, and your heavenly Father knows that you need them. But seek first his kingdom and his righteousness, and all these things will be given to you as well. Therefore do not worry about tomorrow, for tomorrow will worry about itself. Each day has enough trouble of its own.

Matthew 6:25-34 (NIV)

And fear not them which kill the body, but are not able to kill the soul: but rather fear him which is able to destroy both soul and body in hell. Are not two sparrows sold for a farthing? and one of them shall not fall on the ground without your Father. But the very hairs of your head are all numbered. Fear ye not therefore, ye are of more value than many sparrows.

Matthew 10:28-31

Say to them that are of a fearful heart, Be strong, fear not: behold, your God will come with vengeance, even God with a recompence; he will come and save you.

Isaiah 35:4

Have not I commanded thee? Be strong and of a good courage; be not afraid, neither be thou dismayed: for the LORD thy God is with thee whithersoever thou goest.

Joshua 1:9

I called upon the LORD in distress: the LORD answered me, and set me in a large place. The LORD is on my side; I will not fear: what can man do unto me?

Psalm 118:5-6

The fear of man bringeth a snare: but whoso putteth his trust in the LORD shall be safe.

Proverbs 29:25

...Fear ye not, stand still, and see the salvation of the LORD, which he will shew to you to day....

Exodus 14:13

Put not your trust in princes, nor in the son of man, in whom there is no help. His breath goeth forth, he returneth to his earth; in that very day his thoughts perish. Happy is he that hath the God of Jacob for his help, whose hope is in the LORD his God:

Psalm 146:3-5

Though I walk in the midst of trouble, thou wilt revive me: thou shalt stretch forth thine hand against the wrath of mine enemies, and thy right hand shall save me.

Psalm 138:7

I sought the LORD, and he heard me, and delivered me from all my fears.

Psalm 34:4

It is better to trust in the LORD than to put confidence in princes.

Psalm 118:9

Hearken unto me, ye that know righteousness, the people in whose heart is my law; fear ye not the reproach of men, neither be ye afraid of their revilings.

Isaiah 51:7

I will call upon the LORD, who is worthy to be praised: so shall I be saved from mine enemies.

Psalm 18:3

Ye are of God, little children, and have overcome them: because greater is he that is in you, than he that is in the world.

1 John 4:4

The LORD is my light and my salvation; whom shall I fear? the LORD is the strength of my life; of whom shall I be afraid.

Psalm 27:1

There is no fear in love; but perfect love casteth out fear: because fear hath torment. He that feareth is not made perfect in love.

1 John 4:18

But whoever listens to me will live in safety and be at ease, without fear of harm."

Proverbs 1:33 (NIV)

The name of the LORD is a strong tower: the righteous runneth into it, and is safe.

Proverbs 18:10

Healing Scriptures

It is God's will for us to live in divine health; healing is for all who believe. We decide whether to listen to the "facts" or the truth from the Word of God which promised that, "By whose stripes ye were healed" (1 Peter 2:24). *By Jesus dying on the cross, we are redeemed from the curse of sickness and disease.*

We can stand on these promises from God's word for our healing.

Christ hath redeemed us from the curse of the law, being made a curse for us: for it is written, Cursed is every one that hangeth on a tree:

Galatians 3:13

Every good gift and every perfect gift is from above, and cometh down from the Father of lights, with whom is no variableness, neither shadow of turning.

James 1:17

He sent his word, and healed them, and delivered them from their destructions.

Psalm 107:20

My son, attend to my words; incline thine ear unto my sayings. Let them not depart from thine eyes; keep them in the midst of thine heart. For they are life unto those that find them, and health to all their flesh.

Proverbs 4:20-22

And said, If thou wilt diligently hearken to the voice of the LORD thy God, and wilt do that which is right in his sight, and wilt give ear to his commandments, and keep all his statutes, I will put none of these diseases upon thee, which I have brought upon the Egyptians: for I am the LORD that healeth thee.

Exodus 15:26

I call heaven and earth to record this day against you, that I have set before you life and death, blessing and cursing: therefore choose life, that both thou and thy seed may live: That thou mayest love the LORD thy God, and that thou mayest obey his voice, and that thou mayest cleave unto him: for he is thy life, and the length of thy days: that thou mayest dwell in the land which the LORD sware unto thy fathers, to Abraham, to Isaac, and to Jacob, to give them.

Deuteronomy 30:19-20

But unto you that fear my name shall the Sun of righteousness arise with healing in his wings; and ye shall go forth, and grow up as calves of the stall.

Malachi 4:2

Beloved, I wish above all things that thou mayest prosper and be in health, even as thy soul prospereth.

3 John 2

For I will restore health unto thee, and I will heal thee of thy wounds, saith the LORD;

Jeremiah 30:17

And the LORD will take away from thee all sickness, and will put none of the evil diseases of Egypt, which thou knowest, upon thee; but will lay them upon all them that hate thee.

Deuteronomy 7:15

And it shall come to pass in that day, that his burden shall be taken away from off thy shoulder, and his yoke from off thy neck, and the yoke shall be destroyed because of the anointing.

Isaiah 10:27

Surely he hath borne our griefs, and carried our sorrows: yet we did esteem him stricken, smitten of God, and afflicted. But he was wounded for our transgressions, he was bruised for our iniquities: the chastisement of our peace was upon him; and with his stripes we are healed.

Isaiah 53:4-5

And the prayer of faith shall save the sick, and the Lord shall raise him up; and if he have committed sins, they shall be forgiven him. Confess your faults one to another, and pray one for another, that ye may be healed. The effectual fervent prayer of a righteous man availeth much.

James 5:15-16

Turn again, and tell Hezekiah the captain of my people, Thus saith the LORD, the God of David thy father, I have heard thy prayer, I have seen thy tears: behold, I will heal thee: on the third day thou shalt go up unto the house of the LORD.

2 Kings 20:5

Then shall thy light break forth as the morning, and thine health shall spring forth speedily: and thy righteousness shall go before thee; the glory of the LORD shall be thy rearward.

Isaiah 58:8

Behold, I will bring it health and cure, and I will cure them, and will reveal unto them the abundance of peace and truth.

Jeremiah 33:6

How God anointed Jesus of Nazareth with the Holy Ghost and with power: who went about doing good, and healing all that were oppressed of the devil; for God was with him.

Acts 10:38

But if the Spirit of him that raised up Jesus from the dead dwell in you, he that raised up Christ from the dead shall also quicken your mortal bodies by his Spirit that dwelleth in you.

Romans 8:11

And when Jesus departed thence, two blind men followed him, crying, and saying, Thou Son of David, have mercy on us. And when he was come into the house, the blind men came to him: and Jesus saith unto them, Believe ye that I am able to do this? They said unto him, Yea, Lord. Then touched he their eyes, saying, According to your faith be it unto you.

Matthew 9:27-29

And it came to pass, when he was in a certain city, behold a man full of leprosy: who seeing Jesus fell on his face, and besought him, saying, Lord, if thou wilt, thou canst make me clean. And he put forth his hand, and touched him, saying, I will: be thou clean. And immediately the leprosy departed from him.

Luke 5:12-13

And a woman having an issue of blood twelve years, which had spent all her living upon physicians, neither could be healed of any, Came behind him, and touched the border of his garment: and immediately her issue of blood stanched. And Jesus said, Who touched me? When all denied, Peter and they that were with him said, Master, the multitude throng thee and press thee, and sayest thou, Who touched me? And Jesus said, Somebody hath touched me: for I perceive that virtue is gone out of me. And when the woman saw that she was not hid, she came trembling, and falling down before him, she declared unto him before all the people for what cause she had touched him, and how she was healed immediately. And he said unto her, Daughter, be of good comfort: thy faith hath made thee whole; go in peace.

Luke 8:43-48

And one of them smote the servant of the high priest, and cut off his right ear. And Jesus answered and said, Suffer ye thus far. And he touched his ear, and healed him.

Luke 22:50-51

As they went out, behold, they brought to him a dumb man possessed with a devil. And when the devil was cast out, the dumb spake: and the multitudes marveled, saying, It was never so seen in Israel.

Matthew 9:32-33

And when he was departed thence, he went into their synagogue: And, behold, there was a man which had his hand withered. And they asked him, saying, Is it lawful to heal on the Sabbath days? that they might accuse him. And he said unto them, What man shall there be among you, that shall have one sheep, and if it fall into a pit on the Sabbath day, will he not lay hold on it, and lift it out? How much then is a man better than a sheep? Wherefore it is lawful to do well on the Sabbath days. Then saith he to the man, Stretch forth thine hand. And he stretched it forth; and it was restored whole, like as the other.

Matthew 12:9-13

And they came to Jericho: and as he went out of Jericho with his disciples and a great number of people, blind Bartimaeus, the son of Timaeus, sat by the highway side begging. And when he heard that it was Jesus of Nazareth, he began to cry out, and say, Jesus, thou Son of David, have mercy on me. And many charged him that he should hold his peace: but he cried the more a great deal, Thou Son of David, have mercy on me. And Jesus stood still, and commanded him to be called. And they call the blind man, saying unto him, Be of good comfort, rise; he calleth thee. And he, casting away his garment, rose, and came to Jesus. And Jesus answered and said unto him, What wilt thou that I should do unto thee? The blind man said unto him, Lord, that I might receive my sight. And Jesus said unto him, Go thy way; thy faith hath made thee whole. And immediately he received his sight, and followed Jesus in the way.

Mark 10:46-52

Soon afterward, Jesus went to a town called Nain, and his disciples and a large crowd went along with him. As he approached the town gate, a dead person was being carried out—the only son of his mother, and she was a widow. And a large crowd from the town was with her. When the Lord saw her, his heart went out to her and he said, "Don't cry." Then he went up and touched the coffin, and those carrying it stood still. He said, "Young man, I say to you, get up!" The dead man sat up and began to talk, and Jesus gave him back to his mother. They were all filled with awe and praised God. "A great prophet has appeared among us," they said. "God has come to help his people." This news about Jesus spread throughout Judea and the surrounding country.

Luke 7:11-17 (NIV)

And he was teaching in one of the synagogues on the Sabbath. And, behold, there was a woman which had a spirit of infirmity eighteen years, and was bowed together, and could in no wise lift up herself. And when Jesus saw her, he called her to him, and said unto her, Woman, thou art loosed from thine infirmity. And he laid his hands on her: and immediately she was made straight, and glorified God. And the ruler of the synagogue answered with indignation, because that Jesus had healed on the Sabbath day, and said unto the people, There are six days in which men ought to work: in them therefore come and be healed, and not on the Sabbath day. The Lord then answered him, and said, Thou hypocrite, doth not each one of you on the Sabbath loose his ox or his ass from the stall, and lead him away to watering? And ought not this woman, being a daughter of Abraham, whom Satan hath bound, lo, these eighteen years, be loosed from this bond on the Sabbath day?

Luke 13:10-16

And it came to pass, as he went into the house of one of the chief Pharisees to eat bread on the Sabbath day, that they watched him. And, behold, there was a certain man before him which had the dropsy. And

Jesus answering spake unto the lawyers and Pharisees, saying, Is it lawful to heal on the Sabbath day? And they held their peace. And he took him, and healed him, and let him go;

Luke 14:1-4

And it came to pass, as he went to Jerusalem, that he passed through the midst of Samaria and Galilee. And as he entered into a certain village, there met him ten men that were lepers, which stood afar off: And they lifted up their voices, and said, Jesus, Master, have mercy on us. And when he saw them, he said unto them, Go shew yourselves unto the priests. And it came to pass, that, as they went, they were cleansed. And one of them, when he saw that he was healed, turned back, and with a loud voice glorified God, And fell down on his face at his feet, giving him thanks: and he was a Samaritan. And Jesus answering said, Were there not ten cleansed? but where are the nine? There are not found that returned to give glory to God, save this stranger. And he said unto him, Arise, go thy way: thy faith hath made thee whole.

Luke 17:11-19

The royal official said, "Sir, come down before my child dies." Jesus replied, "You may go. Your son will live." The man took Jesus at his word and departed. While he was still on the way, his servants met him with the news that his boy was living. When he inquired as to the time when his son got better, they said to him, "The fever left him yesterday at the seventh hour." Then the father realized that this was the exact time at which Jesus had said to him, "Your son will live." So he and all his household believed.

John 4:49-53 (NIV)

Now there is in Jerusalem by the sheep gate a pool, which is called in Hebrew Bethesda, having five porticoes. In these lay a multitude of those who were sick, blind, lame, and withered, waiting for the moving of the waters; For an angel of the Lord went down at certain seasons into the pool and stirred up the water; whoever then first, after the stirring up of the water, stepped in was made well from whatever disease with which he was afflicted. A man was there who had been ill for thirty-eight years. When Jesus saw him lying there, and knew that he had already been a long time in that condition, He said to him, "Do you wish to get well?" The sick man answered Him, "Sir, I have no man to put me into the pool when the water is stirred up, but while I am coming, another steps down before me." Jesus said to him, "Get up, pick up your pallet and walk." Immediately the man became well, and picked up his pallet and began to walk.

John 5:2-9 (NASB)

And as Jesus passed by, he saw a man which was blind from his birth. And his disciples asked him, saying, Master, who did sin, this man, or his parents, that he was born blind? Jesus answered, Neither hath this man sinned, nor his parents: but that the works of God should be made manifest in him. I must work the works of him that sent me, while it is day: the night cometh, when no man can work. As long as I am in the world, I am the light of the world. When he had thus spoken, he spat on the ground, and made clay of the spittle, and he anointed the eyes of the blind man with the clay, And said unto him, Go, wash in the pool of Siloam, (which is by interpretation, Sent.) He went his way therefore, and washed, and came seeing.

John 9:1-7

Therefore, when Mary came where Jesus was, she saw Him, and fell at His feet, saying to Him, "Lord, if You had been here, my brother would not have died." When Jesus therefore saw her weeping, and the Jews who came with her also weeping, He was deeply moved in spirit and was troubled, and said, "Where have you laid him?" They said to Him, "Lord, come and see." Jesus wept. So the Jews were saying, "See how He loved him!" But some of them said, "Could not this man, who opened the eyes of the blind man, have kept this man also from dying?" So Jesus, again being deeply moved within, came to the tomb. Now it was a cave, and a stone was lying against it. Jesus said, "Remove the stone." Martha, the sister of the deceased, said to Him, "Lord, by this time there will be a stench, for he has been dead four days." Jesus said to her, "Did I not say to you that if you believe, you will see the glory of God?" So they removed the stone. Then Jesus raised His eyes, and said, "Father, I thank You that You have heard Me. I knew that You always hear Me; but because of the people standing around I said it, so that they may believe that You sent Me." When He had said these things, He cried out with a loud voice, "Lazarus, come forth." The man who had died came forth, bound hand and foot with wrappings, and his face was wrapped around with a cloth. Jesus said to them, "Unbind him, and let him go."

John 11:32-44 (NASB)

Ah Lord GOD! behold, thou hast made the heaven and the earth by thy great power and stretched out arm, and there is nothing too hard for thee:

Jeremiah 32:17

And he said unto them, Go ye into all the world, and preach the gospel to every creature. He that believeth and is baptized shall be saved; but he that believeth not shall be damned. And these signs shall follow them that believe; In my name shall they cast out devils; they shall speak with new tongues; They shall take up serpents; and if they drink any deadly thing, it shall not hurt them; they shall lay hands on the sick, and they shall recover. So then after the Lord had spoken unto them, he was received up into heaven, and sat on the right hand of God. And they went forth, and preached every where, the Lord working with them, and confirming the word with signs following. Amen.

Mark 16:15-20

Then Peter said, Silver and gold have I none; but such as I have give I thee: In the name of Jesus Christ of Nazareth rise up and walk. And he took him by the right hand, and lifted him up: and immediately his feet and ankle bones received strength. And he leaping up stood, and walked, and entered with them into the temple, walking, and leaping, and praising God.

Acts 3:6-8

Who his own self bare our sins in his own body on the tree, that we, being dead to sins, should live unto righteousness: by whose stripes ye were healed.

1 Peter 2:24

Verily, verily, I say unto you, He that believeth on me, the works that I do shall he do also; and greater works than these shall he do; because I go unto my Father. And whatsoever ye shall ask in my name, that will I do, that the Father may be glorified in the Son. If ye shall ask any thing in my name, I will do it. If ye love me, keep my commandments.

John 14:12-15

O LORD my God, I cried unto thee, and thou hast healed me.

Psalm 30:2

Bless the LORD, O my soul, and forget not all his benefits Who forgiveth all thine iniquities; who healeth all thy diseases;

Psalm 103:2-3

That thy way may be known upon earth, thy saving health among all nations.

Psalm 67:2

A sound heart is the life of the flesh: but envy the rottenness of the bones.

Proverbs 14:30

A merry heart maketh a cheerful countenance: but by sorrow of the heart the spirit is broken.

Proverbs 15:13

A cheerful look brings joy to the heart, and good news gives health to the bones.

Proverbs 15:30 (NIV)

Pleasant words are a honeycomb, sweet to the soul and healing to the bones.

Proverbs 16:24 (NIV)

Keep thy heart with all diligence; for out of it are the issues of life.

Proverbs 4:23

I shall not die, but live, and declare the works of the LORD.

Psalm 118:17

God's Guidance and Encouragement in Challenging Times

No matter what problems we face in our daily lives, God's Word tells us He is with us and He will never forsake us. His word will guide us, giving us peace and comfort in all of life's situations.

And I will bring the blind by a way that they knew not; I will lead them in paths that they have not known: I will make darkness light before them, and crooked things straight. These things will I do unto them, and not forsake them.

Isaiah 42:16

And thine ears shall hear a word behind thee, saying, This is the way, walk ye in it, when ye turn to the right hand, and when ye turn to the left.

Isaiah 30:21

There shall not any man be able to stand before thee all the days of thy life: as I was with Moses, so I will be with thee: I will not fail thee, nor forsake thee.

Joshua 1:5

...for he hath said, I will never leave thee, nor forsake thee.

Hebrews 13:5

Come unto me, all ye that labour and are heavy laden, and I will give you rest.

Matthew 11:28

Let not your heart be troubled: ye believe in God, believe also in me.

John 14:1

These things I have spoken unto you, that in me ye might have peace. In the world ye shall have tribulation: but be of good cheer; I have overcome the world.

John 16:33

Peace I leave with you, my peace I give unto you: not as the world giveth, give I unto you. Let not your heart be troubled, neither let it be afraid.

John 14:27

God is our refuge and strength, a very present help in trouble.

Psalm 46:1

The LORD is good, a strong hold in the day of trouble; and he knoweth them that trust in him.

Nahum 1:7

Though I walk in the midst of trouble, thou wilt revive me: thou shalt stretch forth thine hand against the wrath of mine enemies, and thy right hand shall save me.

Psalm 138:7

For thou wilt light my candle: the LORD my God will enlighten my darkness. For by thee I have run through a troop; and by my God have I leaped over a wall.

Psalm 18:28-29

Thou art my hiding place; thou shalt preserve me from trouble; thou shalt compass me about with songs of deliverance. Selah.

Psalm 32:7

Many are the afflictions of the righteous: but the LORD delivereth him out of them all.

Psalm 34:19

The LORD upholdeth all that fall, and raiseth up all those that be bowed down.

Psalm 145:14

Truly my soul waiteth upon God: from him cometh my salvation. He only is my rock and my salvation; he is my defense; I shall not be greatly moved. How long will ye imagine mischief against a man? ye shall be slain all of you: as a bowing wall shall ye be, and as a tottering fence. They only consult to cast him down from his excellency: they delight in lies: they bless with their mouth, but they curse inwardly. Selah. My soul, wait thou only upon God; for my expectation is from him. He only is my rock and my salvation: he is my defence; I shall not be moved. In God is my salvation and my glory: the rock of my strength, and my refuge, is in God. Trust in him at all times; ye people, pour out your heart before him: God is a refuge for us. Selah.

Psalm 62:1-8

I will lift up mine eyes unto the hills, from whence cometh my help. My help cometh from the LORD, which made heaven and earth. He will not suffer thy foot to be moved: he that keepeth thee will not slumber. Behold, he that keepeth Israel shall neither slumber nor sleep. The LORD is thy keeper: the LORD is thy shade upon thy right hand. The sun shall not smite thee by day, nor the moon by night. The LORD shall preserve thee from all evil: he shall preserve thy soul. The LORD shall preserve thy going out and thy coming in from this time forth, and even for evermore.

Psalm 121:1-8

For thou wilt not leave my soul in hell; neither wilt thou suffer thine Holy One to see corruption. Thou wilt shew me the path of life: in thy presence is fullness of joy; at thy right hand there are pleasures for evermore.

Psalm 16:10-11

He that dwelleth in the secret place of the most High shall abide under the shadow of the Almighty. I will say of the LORD, He is my refuge and my fortress: my God; in him will I trust. Surely he shall deliver thee from the snare of the fowler, and from the noisome pestilence. He shall cover thee with his feathers, and under his wings shalt thou trust: his truth shall be thy shield and buckler. Thou shalt not be afraid for the terror by night; nor for the arrow that flieth by day; Nor for the pestilence that walketh in darkness; nor for the destruction that wasteth at noonday. A thousand shall fall at thy side, and ten thousand at thy right hand; but it shall not come nigh thee. Only with thine eyes shalt thou behold and see the reward of the wicked. Because thou hast made the LORD, which is my refuge, even the most High, thy habitation; There shall no evil befall thee, neither shall any plague come nigh thy dwelling. For he shall give his angels charge over thee, to keep thee in all thy ways. They shall bear thee up in their hands, lest thou dash thy foot against a stone. Thou shalt tread upon the lion and adder: the young lion and the dragon shalt thou trample under feet. Because he hath set his love upon me, therefore will I deliver him: I will set him on high, because he hath known my name. He shall call upon me, and I will answer him: I will be with him in trouble; I will deliver him, and honour him. With long life will I satisfy him, and shew him my salvation.

Psalm 91:1-16

I have set the LORD always before me: because he is at my right hand, I shall not be moved. Therefore my heart is glad, and my glory rejoiceth: my flesh also shall rest in hope.

Psalm 16:8-9

It is God that girdeth me with strength, and maketh my way perfect. He maketh my feet like hinds' feet, and setteth me upon my high places.

Psalm 18:32-33

I know both how to be abased, and I know how to abound: every where and in all things I am instructed both to be full and to be hungry, both to abound and to suffer need. I can do all things through Christ which strengtheneth me.

Philippians 4:12-13

Then shalt thou walk in thy way safely, and thy foot shall not stumble. When thou liest down, thou shalt not be afraid: yea, thou shalt lie down, and thy sleep shall be sweet. Be not afraid of sudden fear, neither of the desolation of the wicked, when it cometh. For the LORD shall be thy confidence, and shall keep thy foot from being taken.

Proverbs 3:23-26

For surely there is an end; and thine expectation shall not be cut off.

Proverbs 23:18

Return unto thy rest, O my soul; for the LORD hath dealt bountifully with thee.

Psalm 116:7

We are troubled on every side, yet not distressed; we are perplexed, but not in despair; Persecuted, but not forsaken; cast down, but not destroyed; Always bearing about in the body the dying of the Lord Jesus, that the life also of Jesus might be made manifest in our body. For all things are for your sakes, that the abundant grace might through the thanksgiving of many redound to the glory of God. For which cause we faint not; but though our outward man perish, yet the inward man is renewed day by day. For our light affliction, which is but for a moment, worketh for us a far more exceeding and eternal weight of glory; While we look not at the things which are seen, but at the things which are not seen: for the things which are seen are temporal; but the things which are not seen are eternal.

2 Corinthians 4:8-10 & 15-18

When I said, My foot slippeth; thy mercy, O LORD, held me up. In the multitude of my thoughts within me thy comforts delight my soul.

Psalm 94:18-19

Deliver me from mine enemies, O my God: defend me from them that rise up against me. Deliver me from the workers of iniquity, and save me from bloody men. For, lo, they lie in wait for my soul: the mighty are gathered against me; not for my transgression, nor for my sin, O LORD. They run and prepare themselves without my fault: awake to help me, and behold. Thou therefore, O LORD God of hosts, the God of Israel, awake to visit all the heathen: be not merciful to any wicked transgressors. Selah. They return at evening: they make a noise like a dog, and go round about the city. Behold, they belch out with their mouth: swords are in their lips: for who, say they, doth hear? But thou, O LORD, shalt laugh at them; thou shalt have all the heathen in derision. Because of his strength will I wait upon thee: for God is my defence. The God of my mercy shall prevent me: God shall let me see my desire upon mine enemies. Slay them not, lest my people forget: scatter them by thy power; and bring them down, O Lord our shield. For the sin of their mouth and the words of their lips let them even be taken in their pride: and for cursing and lying which they speak. Consume them in wrath, consume them, that they may not be: and let them know that God ruleth in Jacob unto the ends of the earth. Selah. And at evening let them return; and let them make a noise like a dog, and go round about the city. Let them wander up and down for meat, and grudge if they be not satisfied. But I will sing of thy power; yea, I will sing aloud of thy mercy in the morning: for thou hast been my defense and refuge in the day of my trouble. Unto thee, O my strength, will I sing: for God is my defense, and the God of my mercy.

Psalm 59:1-17

He will swallow up death in victory; and the Lord GOD will wipe away tears from off all faces; and the rebuke of his people shall he take away from off all the earth: for the LORD hath spoken it. And it shall be said in that day, Lo, this is our God; we have waited for him, and he will save us: this is the LORD; we have waited for him, we will be glad and rejoice in his salvation.

Isaiah 25:8-9

LORD, how are they increased that trouble me! many are they that rise up against me. Many there be which say of my soul, There is no help for him in God. Selah. But thou, O LORD, art a shield for me; my glory, and the lifter up of mine head. I cried unto the LORD with my voice, and he heard me out of his holy hill. Selah. I laid me down and slept; I awaked; for the LORD sustained me. I will not be afraid of ten thousands of people, that have set themselves against me round about. Arise, O LORD; save me, O my God: for thou hast smitten all mine enemies upon the cheek bone; thou hast broken the teeth of the ungodly. Salvation belongeth unto the LORD: thy blessing is upon thy people. Selah.

Psalm 3:1-8

Because thou hast been my help, therefore in the shadow of thy wings will I rejoice. My soul followeth hard after thee: thy right hand upholdeth me.

Psalm 63:7-8

The Spirit of the Lord GOD is upon me; because the LORD hath anointed me to preach good tidings unto the meek; he hath sent me to bind up the brokenhearted, to proclaim liberty to the captives, and the opening

of the prison to them that are bound; To proclaim
the acceptable year of the LORD, and the day of
vengeance of our God; to comfort all that mourn; To
appoint unto them that mourn in Zion, to give unto
them beauty for ashes, the oil of joy for mourning, the
garment of praise for the spirit of heaviness; that they
might be called trees of righteousness, the planting of
the LORD, that he might be glorified. And they shall
build the old wastes, they shall raise up the former
desolations, and they shall repair the waste cities,
the desolations of many generations. And strangers
shall stand and feed your flocks, and the sons of the
alien shall be your plowmen and your vinedressers.
But ye shall be named the Priests of the LORD: men
shall call you the Ministers of our God: ye shall eat
the riches of the Gentiles, and in their glory shall
ye boast yourselves. For your shame ye shall have
double; and for confusion they shall rejoice in their
portion: therefore in their land they shall possess
the double: everlasting joy shall be unto them. For
I the LORD love judgment, I hate robbery for burnt
offering; and I will direct their work in truth, and I
will make an everlasting covenant with them. And
their seed shall be known among the Gentiles, and
their offspring among the people: all that see them
shall acknowledge them, that they are the seed which
the LORD hath blessed. I will greatly rejoice in the
LORD, my soul shall be joyful in my God; for he
hath clothed me with the garments of salvation, he
hath covered me with the robe of righteousness, as
a bridegroom decketh himself with ornaments, and
as a bride adorneth herself with her jewels. For as
the earth bringeth forth her bud, and as the garden
causeth the things that are sown in it to spring forth;
so the Lord GOD will cause righteousness and praise

to spring forth before all the nations.

Isaiah 61:1-11

Bear ye one another's burdens, and so fulfill the law of Christ.

Galatians 6:2

It is of the LORD's mercies that we are not consumed, because his compassions fail not. They are new every morning: great is thy faithfulness. The LORD is my portion, saith my soul; therefore will I hope in Him.

Lamentations 3:22-24

And Jesus looking upon them saith, With men it is impossible, but not with God: for with God all things are possible.

Mark 10:27

...Is any thing too hard for the LORD?

Genesis 18:14

For the Lamb which is in the midst of the throne shall feed them, and shall lead them unto living fountains of waters: and God shall wipe away all tears from their eyes.

Revelation 7:17

And God shall wipe away all tears from their eyes; and there shall be no more death, neither sorrow, nor crying, neither shall there be any more pain: for the former things are passed away.

Revelation 21:4

Blessings for Obedience

God is always present in our life. His Word never fails us; however, He requires that we obey Him in all things and at all times. This obedience brings great rewards.

"Has the LORD as much delight in burnt offerings and sacrifices as in obeying the voice of the LORD? Behold, to obey is better than sacrifice, And to heed than the fat of rams. "For rebellion is as the sin of divination, And insubordination is as iniquity and idolatry. Because you have rejected the word of the LORD, He has also rejected you from *being* king."

1 Samuel 15:22-23 (NASB)

Jesus said to them, "My food is to do the will of Him who sent Me and to accomplish His work.

John 4:34 (NASB)

I glorified You on the earth, having accomplished the work which You have given Me to do.

John 17:4 (NASB)

If you fully obey the LORD your God and carefully follow all his commands I give you today, the LORD your God will set you high above all the nations on earth. All these blessings will come upon you and accompany you if you obey the LORD your God: You will be blessed in the city and blessed in the country. The fruit of your womb will be blessed, and the crops of your land and the young of your livestock—the calves of your herds and the lambs of your flocks. Your basket and your kneading trough will be blessed. You will be blessed when you come in and blessed when you go out. The LORD will grant that the enemies who rise up against you will be defeated before you. They will come at you from one direction but flee from you in seven. The LORD will send a blessing on your barns and on everything you put your hand to. The LORD your God will bless you in the land he is giving you. The LORD will establish you as his holy people, as he promised you on oath, if you keep the commands of the LORD your God and walk in his ways. Then all the peoples on earth will see that you are called by the name of the LORD, and they will fear you. The LORD will grant you abundant prosperity—in the fruit of your womb, the young of your livestock and the crops of your ground—in the land he swore to your forefathers to give you. The LORD will open the heavens, the storehouse of his bounty, to send rain on your land in season and to bless all the work of your hands. You will lend to many nations but will borrow from none. The LORD will make you the head, not the tail. If you pay attention to the commands of the LORD your God that I give you this day and carefully follow them, you will always be at the top, never at the bottom. Do not turn aside from any of the commands I give you today, to the right or to the left, following other gods and serving them.

Deuteronomy 28:1-14 (NIV)

Now what I am commanding you today is not too difficult for you or beyond your reach. It is not up in heaven, so that you have to ask, "Who will ascend into heaven to get it and proclaim it to us so we may obey it?" Nor is it beyond the sea, so that you have to ask, "Who will cross the sea to get it and proclaim it to us so we may obey it?" No, the word is very near you; it is in your mouth and in your heart so you may obey it. See, I set before you today life and prosperity, death and destruction. For I command you today to love the LORD your God, to walk in his ways, and to keep his commands, decrees and laws; then you will live and increase, and the LORD your God will bless you in the land you are entering to possess. But if your heart turns away and you are not obedient, and if you are drawn away to bow down to other gods and worship them, I declare to you this day that you will certainly be destroyed. You will not live long in the land you are crossing the Jordan to enter and possess. This day I call heaven and earth as witnesses against you that I have set before you life and death, blessings and curses. Now choose life, so that you and your children may live and that you may love the LORD your God, listen to his voice, and hold fast to him. For the LORD is your life, and he will give you many years in the land he swore to give to your fathers, Abraham, Isaac and Jacob.

Deuteronomy 30:11-20 (NIV)

If ye be willing and obedient, ye shall eat the good of the land: But if ye refuse and rebel, ye shall be devoured with the sword: for the mouth of the LORD hath spoken it.

Isaiah 1:19- 20

And I will make of thee a great nation, and I will bless thee, and make thy name great; and thou shalt be a blessing: And I will bless them that bless thee, and curse him that curseth thee: and in thee shall all families of the earth be blessed.

Genesis 12:2-3

And thou shalt do that which is right and good in the sight of the LORD: that it may be well with thee, and that thou mayest go in and possess the good land which the LORD sware unto thy fathers,

Deuteronomy 6:18

If they obey and serve him, they shall spend their days in prosperity, and their years in pleasures.

Job 36:11

Wait on the LORD, and keep his way, and he shall exalt thee to inherit the land: when the wicked are cut off, thou shalt see it.

Psalm 37:34

For thou, LORD, wilt bless the righteous; with favour wilt thou compass him as with a shield.

Psalm 5:12

I have been young, and now am old; yet have I not seen the righteous forsaken, nor his seed begging bread.

Psalm 37:25

What man is he that feareth the LORD? him shall he teach in the way that he shall choose. His soul shall dwell at ease; and his seed shall inherit the earth.

Psalm 25:12-13

If ye walk in my statutes, and keep my commandments, and do them; Then I will give you rain in due season, and the land shall yield her increase, and the trees of the field shall yield their fruit. And your threshing shall reach unto the vintage, and the vintage shall reach unto the sowing time: and ye shall eat your bread to the full, and dwell in your land safely. And I will give peace in the land, and ye shall lie down, and none shall make you afraid: and I will rid evil beasts out of the land, neither shall the sword go through your land. And ye shall chase your enemies, and they shall fall before you by the sword. And five of you shall chase an hundred, and an hundred of you shall put ten thousand to flight: and your enemies shall fall before you by the sword. For I will have respect unto you, and make you fruitful, and multiply you, and establish my covenant with you. And ye shall eat old store, and bring forth the old because of the new. And I will set my tabernacle among you: and my soul shall not abhor you. And I will walk among you, and will be your God, and ye shall be my people. I am the LORD your God, which brought you forth out of the land of Egypt, that ye should not be their bondmen; and I have broken the bands of your yoke, and made you go upright.

Leviticus 26:3-13

And he said, I will make all my goodness pass before thee, and I will proclaim the name of the LORD before thee; and will be gracious to whom I will be gracious, and will shew mercy on whom I will shew mercy.

Exodus 33:19

(The LORD God of your fathers make you a thousand times so many more as ye are, and bless you, as he hath promised you!)

Deuteronomy 1:11

For the LORD thy God hath blessed thee in all the works of thy hand: he knoweth thy walking through

this great wilderness: these forty years the LORD thy
God hath been with thee; thou hast lacked nothing.

Deuteronomy 2:7

Ye shall walk in all the ways which the LORD your
God hath commanded you, that ye may live, and that
it may be well with you, and that ye may prolong your
days in the land which ye shall possess.

Deuteronomy 5:33

I will prevent pests from devouring your crops, and
the vines in your fields will not cast their fruit," says
the LORD Almighty. "Then all the nations will call
you blessed, for yours will be a delightful land," says
the LORD Almighty.

Malachi 3:11-12 (NIV)

His master said to him, 'Well done, good and faithful
slave. You were faithful with a few things, I will put
you in charge of many things; enter into the joy of
your master.'

Matthew 25:21 (NASB)

You will be enriched in everything for all liberality,
which through us is producing thanksgiving to God.

2 Corinthians 9:11 (NASB)

Indeed I will greatly bless you, and I will greatly
multiply your seed as the stars of the heavens and
as the sand which is on the seashore; and your seed
shall possess the gate of their enemies. In your seed
all the nations of the earth shall be blessed, because
you have obeyed My voice."

Genesis 22:17-18 (NASB)

God created man in His own image, in the image of God He created him; male and female He created them. God blessed them; and God said to them, "Be fruitful and multiply, and fill the earth, and subdue it; and rule over the fish of the sea and over the birds of the sky and over every living thing that moves on the earth."

Genesis 1:27-28 (NASB)

God's Principles on Financial Blessings

God is our provider. We can live in abundance in the middle of a world filled with financial crisis. He wants to bless us, but we must follow His instructions and principles from His Word for our financial blessings.

Poverty and shame shall be to him that refuseth instruction: but he that regardeth reproof shall be honoured.

Proverbs 13:18

For even when we were with you, this we commanded you, that if any would not work, neither should he eat.

2 Thessalonians 3:10

But if any provide not for his own, and specially for those of his own house, he hath denied the faith, and is worse than an infidel.

1Timothy 5:8

All hard work brings a profit, but mere talk leads only to poverty.

Proverbs 14:23 (NIV)

Love not sleep, lest thou come to poverty; open thine eyes, and thou shalt be satisfied with bread.

Proverbs 20:13

The sluggard will not plow by reason of the cold; therefore shall he beg in harvest, and have nothing.

Proverbs 20:4

Go to the ant, o sluggard, observe her ways and be wise, Which, having no chief, officer or ruler, Prepares her food in the summer and gathers her provision in the harvest. How long will you lie down, o sluggard? When will you arise from your sleep? "A little sleep, a little slumber, a little folding of the hands to rest" — Your poverty will come in like a vagabond and your need like an armed man.

Proverbs 6:6-11 (NASB)

He who watches the wind will not sow and he who looks at the clouds will not reap. Just as you do not know the path of the wind and how bones are formed in the womb of the pregnant woman, so you do not know the activity of God who makes all things. Sow your seed in the morning and do not be idle in the evening, for you do not know whether morning or evening sowing will succeed, or whether both of them alike will be good.

Ecclesiastes 11:4-6 (NASB)

He who gets wisdom loves his own soul; he who cherishes understanding prospers.

Proverbs 19:8 (NIV)

Who satisfieth thy mouth with good things; so that thy youth is renewed like the eagle's.

Psalm 103:5

Behold, my servant shall deal prudently, he shall be exalted and extolled, and be very high.

Isaiah 52:13

The eyes of all wait upon thee; and thou givest them their meat in due season. Thou openest thine hand, and satisfiest the desire of every living thing.

Psalm 145:15-16

Whatsoever thy hand findeth to do, do it with thy might; for there is no work, nor device, nor knowledge, nor wisdom, in the grave, whither thou goest.

Ecclesiastes 9:10

But seek ye first the kingdom of God, and his righteousness; and all these things shall be added unto you.

Matthew 6:33

Then shalt thou prosper, if thou takest heed to fulfill the statutes and judgments which the LORD charged Moses with concerning Israel: be strong, and of good courage; dread not, nor be dismayed.

1 Chronicles 22:13

Believe in the LORD your God, so shall ye be established; believe his prophets, so shall ye prosper.

2 Chronicles 20:20

Blessed is the man that walketh not in the counsel of the ungodly, nor standeth in the way of sinners, nor sitteth in the seat of the scornful. But his delight is in the law of the LORD; and in his law doth he meditate day and night. And he shall be like a tree planted by the rivers of water, that bringeth forth his fruit in his season; his leaf also shall not wither; and whatsoever he doeth shall prosper.

Psalm 1:1-3

Beloved, I wish above all things that thou mayest prosper and be in health, even as thy soul prospereth.

3 John 2

I, even I, have spoken; yea, I have called him: I have brought him, and he shall make his way prosperous.

Isaiah 48:15

Let them shout for joy, and be glad, that favour my righteous cause: yea, let them say continually, Let the LORD be magnified, which hath pleasure in the prosperity of his servant.

Psalm 35:27

The thief cometh not, but for to steal, and to kill, and to destroy: I am come that they might have life, and that they might have it more abundantly.

John 10:10

But my God shall supply all your need according to his riches in glory by Christ Jesus.

Philippians 4:19

And the LORD was with Joseph, and he was a prosperous man; and he was in the house of his master the Egyptian. And Joseph found grace in his sight, and he served him: and he made him overseer over his house, and all that he had he put into his hand.

Genesis 39:2 & 4

The LORD maketh poor, and maketh rich: he bringeth low, and lifteth up. He raiseth up the poor out of the dust, and lifteth up the beggar from the dunghill, to set them among princes, and to make them inherit the throne of glory: for the pillars of the earth are the LORD'S, and he hath set the world upon them. He will keep the feet of his saints, and the wicked shall be silent in darkness; for by strength shall no man prevail.

1 Samuel 2:7-9

Seest thou a man diligent in his business? he shall stand before kings; he shall not stand before mean men.

Proverbs 22:29

But thou shalt remember the LORD thy God: for it is he that giveth thee power to get wealth, that he may establish his covenant which he sware unto thy fathers, as it is this day.

Deuteronomy 8:18

For promotion cometh neither from the east, nor from the west, nor from the south. But God is the judge: he putteth down one, and setteth up another.

Psalm 75:6-7

Giving and Receiving

When we give to God, we are tapping into His supernatural fountain of blessing. God does not need our money but we need His blessing.

The earth is the LORD'S, and the fullness thereof; the world, and they that dwell therein.

Psalm 24:1

The silver is mine, and the gold is mine, saith the LORD of hosts.

Haggai 2:8

The sea is his, and he made it: and his hands formed the dry land.

Psalm 95:5

"I shall take no young bull out of your house nor male goats out of your folds. For every beast of the forest is Mine, The cattle on a thousand hills. I know every bird of the mountains, and everything that moves in the field is Mine. If I were hungry I would not tell you, for the world is Mine, and all it contains.

Psalm 50:9-12 (NASB)

Honour the LORD with thy substance, and with the firstfruits of all thine increase: So shall thy barns be filled with plenty, and thy presses shall burst out with new wine.

Proverbs 3:9-10

And now, behold, I have brought the firstfruits of the land, which thou, O LORD, hast given me. And thou shalt set it before the LORD thy God, and worship before the LORD thy God:

Deuteronomy 26:10

Give unto the LORD the glory due unto his name: bring an offering, and come into his courts.

Psalm 96:8

And none shall appear before me empty. The first of the firstfruits of thy land thou shalt bring unto the house of the LORD thy God. Thou shalt not seethe a kid in his mother's milk.

Exodus 34:20 & 26

Every man shall give as he is able, according to the blessing of the LORD your God which He has given you.

Deuteronomy 16:17 (NASB)

Now this I say, he who sows sparingly will also reap sparingly, and he who sows bountifully will also reap bountifully. Each one must do just as he has purposed in his heart, not grudgingly or under compulsion, for God loves a cheerful giver. And God is able to make all grace abound to you, so that always having all sufficiency in everything, you may have an abundance for every good deed.

2 Corinthians 9:6-8 (NASB)

Give, and it shall be given unto you; good measure, pressed down, and shaken together, and running over, shall men give into your bosom. For with the same measure that ye mete withal it shall be measured to you again.

Luke 6:38

He that hath pity upon the poor lendeth unto the
LORD; and that which he hath given will he pay him
again.

Proverbs 19:17

I have shewed you all things, how that so labouring
ye ought to support the weak, and to remember the
words of the Lord Jesus, how he said, It is more
blessed to give than to receive.

Acts 20:35

He that giveth unto the poor shall not lack: but he that
hideth his eyes shall have many a curse.

Proverbs 28:27

The righteous shall flourish like the palm tree: he
shall grow like a cedar in Lebanon.

Psalm 92:12

(As it is written, He hath dispersed abroad; he hath
given to the poor: his righteousness remaineth for
ever. Now he that ministereth seed to the sower both
minister bread for your food, and multiply your seed
sown, and increase the fruits of your righteousness;)

2 Corinthians 9:9-10

So when you give to the needy, do not announce it
with trumpets, as the hypocrites do in the synagogues
and on the streets, to be honored by men. I tell you
the truth, they have received their reward in full. But
when you give to the needy do not let your left hand
know what your right hand is doing, so that your
giving may be in secret. Then your Father, who sees
what is done in secret, will reward you.

Matthew 6:2-4 (NIV)

There is that scattereth, and yet increaseth; and there is that withholdeth more than is meet, but it tendeth to poverty. The liberal soul shall be made fat: and he that watereth shall be watered also himself. He that withholdeth corn, the people shall curse him: but blessing shall be upon the head of him that selleth it.

Proverbs 11:24-26

Will a man rob God? Yet ye have robbed me. But ye say, Wherein have we robbed thee? In tithes and offerings. Ye are cursed with a curse: for ye have robbed me, even this whole nation. Bring ye all the tithes into the storehouse, that there may be meat in mine house, and prove me now herewith, saith the LORD of hosts, if I will not open you the windows of heaven, and pour you out a blessing, that there shall not be room enough to receive it. And I will rebuke the devourer for your sakes, and he shall not destroy the fruits of your ground; neither shall your vine cast her fruit before the time in the field, saith the LORD of hosts. And all nations shall call you blessed: for ye shall be a delightsome land, saith the LORD of hosts.

Malachi 3:8-12

Heal the sick, raise the dead, cleanse the lepers, cast out demons. Freely you received, freely give.

Matthew 10:8 (NASB)

GOD'S WORD FOR HOME AND FAMILY

Wisdom from the Word of God for Building a Godly Home

Home should be a haven of love with a proper line of authority, love, and respect shown among the family members. Home is where we train the character of our future pastors, missionaries, evangelists, teachers, presidents, doctors, lawyers, and many other professions. With God's help, we can nurture our children to become all that God has made them to be, laying a foundation built upon God's precepts. Most importantly, by making God the Head of our household, we are sure to succeed!

...but as for me and my house, we will serve the LORD.

Joshua 24:15

Nevertheless let every one of you in particular so love his wife even as himself; and the wife see that she reverence her husband.

Ephesians 5:33

Husbands, love your wives, even as Christ also loved the church, and gave himself for it; So ought men to love their wives as their own bodies. He that loveth his wife loveth himself.

Ephesians 5:25 & 28

In the same way, you wives, be submissive to
your own husbands so that even if any of them are
disobedient to the word, they may be won without a
word by the behavior of their wives, as they observe
your chaste and respectful behavior. Your adornment
must not be merely external—braiding the hair,
and wearing gold jewelry, or putting on dresses;
but let it be the hidden person of the heart, with the
imperishable quality of a gentle and quiet spirit,
which is precious in the sight of God. For in this way
in former times the holy women also, who hoped in
God, used to adorn themselves, being submissive to
their own husbands; just as Sarah obeyed Abraham,
calling him lord, and you have become her children if
you do what is right without being frightened by any
fear. You husbands in the same way, live with your
wives in an understanding way, as with someone
weaker, since she is a woman; and show her honor as
a fellow heir of the grace of life, so that your prayers
will not be hindered.

1 Peter 3:1-7 (NASB)

Nevertheless neither is the man without the woman,
neither the woman without the man, in the Lord. For
as the woman is of the man, even so is the man also
by the woman; but all things of God.

1 Corinthians 11:11-12

Wives, submit yourselves unto your own husbands,
as unto the Lord. For the husband is the head of the
wife, even as Christ is the head of the church: and he
is the saviour of the body. Therefore as the church is

subject unto Christ, so let the wives be to their own husbands in every thing.

Ephesians 5:22-24

Two are better than one; because they have a good reward for their labour. For if they fall, the one will lift up his fellow: but woe to him that is alone when he falleth; for he hath not another to help him up. Again, if two lie together, then they have heat: but how can one be warm alone?

Ecclesiastes 4:9-11

For none of us liveth to himself, and no man dieth to himself.

Romans 14:7

Children, obey your parents in the Lord: for this is right. Honour thy father and mother; (which is the first commandment with promise;) That it may be well with thee, and thou mayest live long on the earth.

Ephesians 6:1-3

Honour thy father and thy mother, as the LORD thy God hath commanded thee; that thy days may be prolonged, and that it may go well with thee, in the land which the LORD thy God giveth thee.

Deuteronomy 5:16

Finally, be ye all of one mind, having compassion one of another, love as brethren, be pitiful, be courteous: Not rendering evil for evil, or railing for railing: but contrariwise blessing; knowing that ye are thereunto called, that ye should inherit a blessing. For he that will love life, and see good days, let him refrain his tongue from evil, and his lips that they speak no guile:

Let him eschew evil, and do good; let him seek peace, and ensue it.

1 Peter 3:8-11

Let love be without dissimulation. Abhor that which is evil; cleave to that which is good. Be kindly affectioned one to another with brotherly love; in honour preferring one another;

Romans 12:9-10

Follow peace with all men, and holiness, without which no man shall see the Lord:

Hebrews 12:14

And we beseech you, brethren, to know them which labour among you, and are over you in the Lord, and admonish you; And to esteem them very highly in love for their work's sake. And be at peace among yourselves. Now we exhort you, brethren, warn them that are unruly, comfort the feebleminded, support the weak, be patient toward all men. See that none render evil for evil unto any man; but ever follow that which is good, both among yourselves, and to all men. Rejoice evermore. Pray without ceasing. In every thing give thanks: for this is the will of God in Christ Jesus concerning you. Quench not the Spirit. Despise not prophesyings. Prove all things; hold fast that which is good. Abstain from all appearance of evil. And the very God of peace sanctify you wholly; and I pray God your whole spirit and soul and body be preserved blameless unto the coming of our Lord Jesus Christ. Faithful is he that calleth you, who also will do it.

1 Thessalonians 5:13-24

Speaking to yourselves in psalms and hymns and spiritual songs, singing and making melody in your heart to the Lord; Giving thanks always for all things unto God and the Father in the name of our Lord Jesus Christ; Submitting yourselves one to another in the fear of God.

Ephesians 5:19-21

Know therefore today, and take it to your heart, that the LORD, He is God in heaven above and on the earth below; there is no other. So you shall keep His statutes and His commandments which I am giving you today, that it may go well with you and with your children after you, and that you may live long on the land which the LORD your God is giving you for all time."

Deuteronomy 4:39-40 (NASB)

The house of the wicked shall be overthrown: but the tabernacle of the upright shall flourish.

Proverbs 14:11

Except the LORD build the house, they labour in vain that build it: except the LORD keep the city, the watchman waketh but in vain. It is vain for you to rise up early, to sit up late, to eat the bread of sorrows: for so he giveth his beloved sleep.

Psalm 127:1-2

O that there were such an heart in them, that they would fear me, and keep all my commandments always, that it might be well with them, and with their children for ever!

Deuteronomy 5:29

The wicked desireth the net of evil men: but the root of the righteous yieldeth fruit. The wicked is snared by the transgression of his lips: but the just shall come out of trouble. A man shall be satisfied with good by the fruit of his mouth: and the recompence of a man's hands shall be rendered unto him.

Proverbs 12:12-14

And thou shalt love the LORD thy God with all thine heart, and with all thy soul, and with all thy might. And these words, which I command thee this day, shall be in thine heart: And thou shalt teach them diligently unto thy children, and shalt talk of them when thou sittest in thine house, and when thou walkest by the way, and when thou liest down, and when thou risest up. And thou shalt bind them for a sign upon thine hand, and they shall be as frontlets between thine eyes. And thou shalt write them upon the posts of thy house, and on thy gates.

Deuteronomy 6:5-9

Even them will I bring to my holy mountain, and make them joyful in my house of prayer: their burnt offerings and their sacrifices shall be accepted upon mine altar; for mine house shall be called an house of prayer for all people.

Isaiah 56:7

The fear of the LORD tendeth to life: and he that hath it shall abide satisfied; he shall not be visited with evil.

Proverbs 19:23

So you will walk in the way of good men and keep to the paths of the righteous. For the upright will live in the land and the blameless will remain in it;

But the wicked will be cut off from the land and the treacherous will be uprooted from it.

Proverbs 2:20-22 (NASB)

In the fear of the LORD is strong confidence: and his children shall have a place of refuge.

Proverbs 14:26

Or how can anyone enter the strong man's house and carry off his property, unless he first binds the strong *man*? And then he will plunder his house.

Matthew 12:29 (NASB)

It is to a man's honor to avoid strife, but every fool is quick to quarrel.

Proverbs 20:3 (NIV)

And my people shall dwell in a peaceable habitation, and in sure dwellings, and in quiet resting places;

Isaiah 32:18

When a man's ways please the LORD, he maketh even his enemies to be at peace with him.

Proverbs 16:7

He that followeth after righteousness and mercy findeth life, righteousness, and honour.

Proverbs 21:21

And their seed shall be known among the Gentiles, and their offspring among the people: all that see them shall acknowledge them, that they are the seed which the LORD hath blessed.

Isaiah 61:9

Surely his salvation is nigh them that fear him; that glory may dwell in our land. Mercy and truth are met together; righteousness and peace have kissed each other. Truth shall spring out of the earth; and righteousness shall look down from heaven. Yea, the LORD shall give that which is good; and our land shall yield her increase. Righteousness shall go before him; and shall set us in the way of his steps.

Psalm 85:9-13

The fear of the LORD is the instruction of wisdom; and before honour is humility.

Proverbs 15:33

By humility and the fear of the LORD are riches, and honour, and life.

Proverbs 22:4

Pride goeth before destruction, and an haughty spirit before a fall.

Proverbs 16:18

Iron sharpeneth iron; so a man sharpeneth the countenance of his friend.

Proverbs 27:17

Let him know, that he which converteth the sinner from the error of his way shall save a soul from death, and shall hide a multitude of sins.

James 5:20

Better is a dinner of herbs where love is, than a stalled ox and hatred therewith.

Proverbs 15:17

Hatred stirreth up strifes: but love covereth all sins.

Proverbs 10:12

Behold, how good and how pleasant it is for brethren to dwell together in unity!

Psalm 133:1

Above all, love each other deeply, because love covers over a multitude of sins.

1 Peter 4:8 (NIV)

Marriage is a Covenant with God

God desires for a husband and wife to be united in one spirit. Strife brings defeat to us and our family, but unity will bring victory. There is no greater power on earth than the power of agreement between husband and wife. "Any kingdom filled with civil war is doomed; so is a home filled with argument and strife." (Luke 11:17) *The enemy cannot touch our family when we make God the center of our marriage and we are united as one. We need to learn to work with our spouse as one team. Marriage is not to endure but to enjoy and it should manifest the life of Christ on earth.*

And the LORD God caused a deep sleep to fall upon Adam, and he slept: and he took one of his ribs, and closed up the flesh instead thereof; And the rib, which the LORD God had taken from man, made he a woman, and brought her unto the man. And Adam said, This is now bone of my bones, and flesh of my flesh: she shall be called Woman, because she was taken out of Man. Therefore shall a man leave his father and his mother, and shall cleave unto his wife: and they shall be one flesh.

Genesis 2:21-24

"Haven't you read," he replied, "that at the beginning the Creator 'made them male and female,' and said, 'For this reason a man will leave his father and mother and be united to his wife, and the two will become one flesh' So they are no longer two, but one. Therefore what God has joined together, let man not separate."

Matthew 19:4-6 (NIV)

And if one prevail against him, two shall withstand him; and a threefold cord is not quickly broken.

Ecclesiastes 4:12

Or else how can one enter into a strong man's house, and spoil his goods, except he first bind the strong man? and then he will spoil his house."

Matthew 12:29

House and riches are the inheritance of fathers: and a prudent wife is from the LORD.

Proverbs 19:14

He who finds a wife finds a good thing and obtains favor from the LORD.

Proverbs 18:22 (NASB)

Every kingdom divided against itself is brought to desolation; and a house divided against a house falleth.

Luke 11:17

Again I say unto you, That if two of you shall agree on earth as touching any thing that they shall ask, it shall be done for them of my Father which is in heaven. For where two or three are gathered together in my name, there am I in the midst of them.

Matthew 18:19-20

Responsibilities in Marriage

We must keep our marriage pure and holy and never stop loving each other.

Marriage is to be held in honor among all, and the marriage bed is to be undefiled; for fornicators and adulterers God will judge.

Hebrews 13:4 (NASB)

Flee fornication. Every sin that a man doeth is without the body; but he that committeth fornication sinneth against his own body.

1 Corinthians 6:18

Nevertheless, to avoid fornication, let every man have his own wife, and let every woman have her own husband. Let the husband render unto the wife due benevolence: and likewise also the wife unto the husband. The wife hath not power of her own body, but the husband: and likewise also the husband hath not power of his own body, but the wife. Defraud ye not one the other, except it be with consent for a time, that ye may give yourselves to fasting and prayer; and come together again, that Satan tempt you not for your incontinency. But I speak this by permission, and not of commandment.

1 Corinthians 7:2-6

Neither let us commit fornication, as some of them committed, and fell in one day three and twenty thousand.

1 Corinthians 10:8

For this is the will of God, even your sanctification,
that ye should abstain from fornication:

1 Thessalonians 4:3

But I say unto you, That whosoever shall put away his
wife, saving for the cause of fornication, causeth her
to commit adultery: and whosoever shall marry her
that is divorced committeth adultery.

Matthew 5:32

But fornication, and all uncleanness, or covetousness,
let it not be once named among you, as becometh
saints; Neither filthiness, nor foolish talking, nor
jesting, which are not convenient: but rather giving
of thanks. For this ye know, that no whoremonger,
nor unclean person, nor covetous man, who is an
idolater, hath any inheritance in the kingdom of
Christ and of God.

Ephesians 5:3-5

Now the works of the flesh are manifest, which
are these; Adultery, fornication, uncleanness,
lasciviousness, Idolatry, witchcraft, hatred, variance,
emulations, wrath, strife, seditions, heresies,
Envyings, murders, drunkenness, revellings, and
such like: of the which I tell you before, as I have also
told you in time past, that they which do such things
shall not inherit the kingdom of God.

Galatians 5:19-21

Mortify therefore your members which are upon the
earth; fornication, uncleanness, inordinate affection,
evil concupiscence, and covetousness, which is
idolatry:

Colossians 3:5

But that we write unto them, that they abstain from pollutions of idols, and from fornication,

Acts 15:20

Even as Sodom and Gomorrah, and the cities about them in like manner, giving themselves over to fornication, and going after strange flesh, are set forth for an example, suffering the vengeance of eternal fire.

Jude 7

Let thy fountain be blessed: and rejoice with the wife of thy youth. Let her be as the loving hind and pleasant roe;

Proverbs 5:18-19

Live joyfully with the wife whom thou lovest all the days of the life of thy vanity, which he hath given thee under the sun, all the days of thy vanity: for that is thy portion in this life, and in thy labour which thou takest under the sun.

Ecclesiastes 9:9

Many waters cannot quench love, neither can the floods drown it: if a man would give all the substance of his house for love, it would utterly be contemned.

Song of Solomon 8:7

Wisdom for Parents to Raise Godly Children

1. Be a good role model for your children.

A student is not above his teacher, but everyone who is fully trained will be like his teacher.

Luke 6:40 (NIV)

2. Make prayer with your children a part of your daily life.

But seek ye first the kingdom of God, and his righteousness; and all these things shall be added unto you.

Matthew 6:33

And thou shalt teach them diligently unto thy children, and shalt talk of them when thou sittest in thine house, and when thou walkest by the way, and when thou liest down, and when thou risest up. And thou shalt bind them for a sign upon thine hand, and they shall be as frontlets between thine eyes. And thou shalt write them upon the posts of thy house, and on thy gates.

Deuteronomy 6:7-9

3. Treat children as treasured possessions from God.

The Lord your God has chosen you out of all the peoples on the face of the earth to be his people, his treasured possession.

Deuteronomy 7:6 (NIV)

4. Teach your children about the reverential fear of God.

Reverence for God gives a man deep strength; his children have a place of refuge and security.

Proverbs 14:26 (TLB)

The fear of the LORD adds length to life, but the years of the wicked are cut short.

Proverbs 10:27 (NIV)

The fear of the LORD is the beginning of wisdom: and the knowledge of the holy is understanding. For by me thy days shall be multiplied, and the years of thy life shall be increased

Proverbs 9:10-11

Now all has been heard; here is the conclusion of the matter: Fear God and keep his commandments, for this is the duty of all mankind.

Ecclesiastes 12:13 (NIV)

5. Teach your children to honor you, parents, so it may go well with them.

Honour thy father and thy mother, as the LORD thy God hath commanded thee; that thy days may be prolonged, and that it may go well with thee, in the land which the LORD thy God giveth thee."

Deuteronomy 5:16

Children, obey your parents in the Lord: for this is right. Honour thy father and mother; which is the first commandment with promise; That it may be well with thee, and thou mayest live long on the earth.

Ephesians 6:1-3

6. Teach them diligently to obey God, whom you love.

Love the LORD your God with all your heart and with all your soul and with all your strength. These commandments that I give you today are to be on your hearts. Impress them on your children. Talk about them when you sit at home and when you walk along the road, when you lie down and when you get up. Tie them as symbols on your hands and bind them on your foreheads. Write them on the doorframes of your houses and on your gates.

Deuteronomy 6:5-9 (NIV)

7. Help them to grow daily in the Lord and to attain an intimate relationship with Jesus Christ.

Train up a child in the way he should go: and when he is old, he will not depart from it.

Proverbs 22:6

And that from a child thou hast known the holy scriptures, which are able to make thee wise unto salvation through faith which is in Christ Jesus.

2 Timothy 3:15

My son, attend to my words; incline thine ear unto my sayings. Let them not depart from thine eyes; keep them in the midst of thine heart. For they are life unto those that find them, and health to all their flesh.

Proverbs 4:20-22

That ye might walk worthy of the Lord unto all pleasing, being fruitful in every good work, and increasing in the knowledge of God;

Colossians 1:10

For this reason I kneel before the father, from whom his whole family in heaven and on earth derives its name. I pray that out of his glorious riches he may strengthen you with power through his Spirit in you inner being, so that Christ may dwell in your hearts through faith. And I pray that you, being rooted and established in love, may have power, together with all saints, to grasp how wide and long and high and deep is the love of Christ, and to know this love that surpassed knowledge -- that you may be filled to the measure of all the fullness of God.

Ephesians 1:14-19

8. Teach your children to respect, honor, and pray for all that are in authority.

I exhort therefore, that, first of all, supplications, prayers, intercessions, and giving of thanks, be made for all men; For kings, and for all that are in authority; that we may lead a quiet and peaceable life in all godliness and honesty.

1Timothy 2:1-2

Young men, follow the lead of those who are older. All of you, put on a spirit that is free of pride toward each other as if it were your clothes. Scripture says, "God opposes those who are proud. But he gives grace to those who are not." So don't be proud. Put yourselves under God's mighty hand. Then he will honor you at the right time.

1 Peter 5:5-6 (NIV)

9. Teach your children to be accountable and responsible for their words, attitudes, and actions. True love disciplines them God's way.

So then, each of us will give an account of ourselves to God.
>   Romans 14:12 (NIV)

For God will bring every deed into judgment, including every hidden thing, whether it is good or evil.
>   Ecclesiastes 12:14 (NIV)

But I tell you that everyone will have to give account on the day of judgment for every empty word they have spoken.
>   Matthew 12:36 (NIV)

Truthful lips endure forever, but a lying tongue lasts only a moment.
>   Proverbs 12:19 (NIV)

Words from the mouth of the wise are gracious, but fools are consumed by their own lips.
>   Ecclesiastes 10:12 (NIV)

Do not let your mouth lead you into sin.
>   Ecclesiastes 5:6 (NIV)

When words are many, sin is not absent, but he who holds his tongue is wise.
>   Proverbs 10:19 (NIV)

The lips of the righteous nourish many, but fools die for lack of sense.
>   Proverbs 10:21 (NIV)

Even small children are known by their actions, so is
their conduct really pure and upright?

Proverbs 20:11 (NIV)

Be sure of this: The wicked will not go unpunished,
but those who are righteous will go free.

Proverbs 11:21(NIV)

The Lord disciplines the one he loves, and he chastens
everyone he accepts as his son."

Hebrews 12:6 (NIV)

Whoever spares the rod hates their children, but the one
who loves their children is careful to discipline them.

Proverbs 13:24 (NIV)

Folly is bound up in the heart of a child, but the rod of
discipline will drive it far away.

Proverbs 22:15 (NIV)

Discipline your children, and they will give you
peace; they will bring you the delights you desire.

Proverbs 29:17 (NIV)

Do not withhold discipline from a child; if you punish
them with the rod, they will not die.

Proverbs 23:13 (NIV)

A wise son heeds his father's instruction, but a mocker
does not respond to rebukes.

Proverbs 13:1 (NIV)

A rod and a reprimand impart wisdom, but a child left
undisciplined disgraces its mother.

Proverbs 29:15 (NIV)

Discipline your children, for in that there is hope; do not be a willing party to their death.
Proverbs 19:18 (NIV)

Whoever disregards discipline comes to poverty and shame, but whoever heeds correction is honored.
Proverbs 13:18 (NIV)

No discipline seems pleasant at the time, but painful. Later on, however, it produces a harvest of righteousness and peace for those who have been trained by it.
Hebrews 12:11 (NIV)

...for whatsoever a man soweth, that shall he also reap. And let us not be weary in well doing: for in due season we shall reap, if we faint not.
Galatians 6:7-9

10. Provide consistent healthy boundaries for your children.

He that hath no rule over his own spirit is like a city that is broken down, and without walls.
Proverbs 25:28

He that walketh with wise men shall be wise: but a companion of fools shall be destroyed.
Proverbs 13:20

11. Teach them to walk in integrity.

May integrity and uprightness protect me, because

161

my hope, LORD, is in you.

Psalm 25:21 (NIV)

"As for you, if you walk before me faithfully with integrity of heart and uprightness, as David your father did, and do all I command and observe my decrees and laws, I will establish your royal throne over Israel forever, as I promised David your father when I said, 'You shall never fail to have a successor on the throne of Israel.'

1 Kings 9:4-5 (NIV)

Whoever walks in integrity walks securely, but whoever takes crooked paths will be found out.

Proverbs 10:9 (NIV)

The integrity of the upright guides them, but the unfaithful are destroyed by their duplicity.

Proverbs 11:3 (NIV)

You who are young, be happy while you are young, and let your heart give you joy in the days of your youth. Follow the ways of your heart and whatever your eyes see, but know that for all these things God will bring you into judgment.

Ecclesiastes 11:9 (NIV)

For this reason, since the day we heard about you, we have not stopped praying for you. We continually ask God to fill you with the knowledge of his will through all the wisdom and understanding that the Spirit gives, So that you may live a life worthy of the Lord and please him in every way: bearing fruit in every good work, growing in the knowledge of God,

Colossians 1:9-10 (NIV)

12. Train, teach, and reinforce godly character.

All scripture is given by inspiration of God, and is profitable for doctrine, for reproof, for correction, for instruction in righteousness: That the man of God may be perfect, thoroughly furnished unto all good works.

2 Timothy 3:16-17

My son, attend to my words; incline thine ear unto my sayings. Let them not depart from thine eyes; keep them in the midst of thine heart. For they are life unto those that find them, and health to all their flesh.

Proverbs 4:20-22

13. Memorize scriptures with them.

Thy word have I hid in mine heart, that I might not sin against thee.

Psalm 119:11

And how from infancy you have known the Holy Scriptures, which are able to make you wise for salvation through faith in Christ Jesus.

2 Timothy 3:15 (NIV)

14. Speak blessings, visions and dreams into your children's life.

Death and life are in the power of the tongue: and they that love it shall eat the fruit thereof.

Proverbs 18:21

My people are destroyed for lack of knowledge:

Hosea 4:6

15. Impart into your children spiritual values. These are some of the spiritual values you can start with, commitment to the church, giving of tithes, offerings, caring for elderly, and serving others.

Be not deceived; God is not mocked: for whatsoever a man soweth, that shall he also reap. For he that soweth to his flesh shall of the flesh reap corruption; but he that soweth to the Spirit shall of the Spirit reap life everlasting. And let us not be weary in well doing: for in due season we shall reap, if we faint not.

Galatians 6:7-9

16. Take responsibility for the influences of your child's life; for example, friends, activities, TV, music, etc.

Keep thy heart with all diligence; for out of it are the issues of life.

Proverbs 4:23

17. Time with your children is an investment. Spend quality and quantity time with your children.

Someone said, "All the money in the world cannot take your place in your child's life."

Lay not up for yourselves treasures upon earth, where moth and rust doth corrupt, and where thieves break through and steal: But lay up for yourselves treasures in heaven, where neither moth nor rust doth corrupt, and where thieves do not break through nor steal: For where your treasure is, there will your heart be also.

Matthew 6:19-21

Lo, children are an heritage of the LORD: and the fruit of the womb is his reward. As arrows are in the hand of a mighty man; so are children of the youth. Happy is the man that hath his quiver full of them: they shall not be ashamed, but they shall speak with the enemies in the gate.

Psalm 127:3-5

And their seed shall be known among the Gentiles, and their offspring among the people: all that see them shall acknowledge them, that they are the seed which the LORD hath blessed.

Isaiah 61:9

But Jesus called them unto him, and said, Suffer little children to come unto me, and forbid them not: for of such is the kingdom of God.

Luke 18:16

Husband's Prayer for Wife

Who can find a virtuous woman? for her price is far above rubies. The heart of her husband doth safely trust in her, so that he shall have no need of spoil. She will do him good and not evil all the days of her life. She seeketh wool, and flax, and worketh willingly with her hands. She is like the merchants' ships; she bringeth her food from afar. She riseth also while it is yet night, and giveth meat to her household, and a portion to her maidens. She considereth a field, and buyeth it: with the fruit of her hands she planteth a vineyard. She girdeth her loins with strength, and strengtheneth her arms. She perceiveth that her merchandise is good: her candle goeth not out by night. She layeth her hands to the spindle, and her hands hold the distaff. She stretcheth out her hand to the poor; yea, she reacheth forth her hands to the needy. She is not afraid of the snow for her household: for all her household are clothed with scarlet. She maketh herself coverings of tapestry; her clothing is silk and purple. Her husband is known in the gates, when he sitteth among the elders of the land. She maketh fine linen, and selleth it; and delivereth girdles unto the merchant. Strength and honour are her clothing; and she shall rejoice in time to come. She openeth her mouth with wisdom; and in her tongue is the law of kindness. She looketh well to the ways of her household, and eateth not the bread of idleness. Her children arise up, and call her blessed; her husband also, and he praiseth her. Many daughters have done virtuously, but thou excellest them all. Favour is deceitful, and beauty is vain: but a woman that feareth the LORD, she shall be praised. Give her of the fruit of her hands; and let her own works praise her in the gates.

Proverbs 31:10-31

Wife's Prayer for Husband

Praise ye the LORD. Blessed is the man that feareth the LORD, that delighteth greatly in his commandments. His seed shall be mighty upon earth: the generation of the upright shall be blessed. Wealth and riches shall be in his house: and his righteousness endureth for ever. Unto the upright there ariseth light in the darkness: he is gracious, and full of compassion, and righteous. A good man sheweth favour, and lendeth: he will guide his affairs with discretion. Surely he shall not be moved for ever: the righteous shall be in everlasting remembrance. He shall not be afraid of evil tidings: his heart is fixed, trusting in the LORD. His heart is established, he shall not be afraid, until he see his desire upon his enemies. He hath dispersed, he hath given to the poor; his righteousness endureth for ever; his horn shall be exalted with honour. The wicked shall see it, and be grieved; he shall gnash with his teeth, and melt away: the desire of the wicked shall perish.

Psalm 112:1-10

Blessed is every one that feareth the LORD; that walketh in his ways. For thou shalt eat the labour of thine hands: happy shalt thou be, and it shall be well with thee. Thy wife shall be as a fruitful vine by the sides of thine house: thy children like olive plants round about thy table. Behold, that thus shall the man be blessed that feareth the LORD. The LORD shall bless thee out of Zion: and thou shalt see the good of Jerusalem all the days of thy life. Yea, thou shalt see thy children's children, and peace upon Israel.

Psalm 128:1-6

Blessed is the man that walketh not in the counsel of the ungodly, nor standeth in the way of sinners, nor sitteth in the seat of the scornful. But his delight is in the law of the LORD; and in his law doth he meditate day and night. And he shall be like a tree planted by the rivers of water, that bringeth forth his fruit in his season; his leaf also shall not wither; and whatsoever he doeth shall prosper. The ungodly are not so: but are like the chaff which the wind driveth away. Therefore the ungodly shall not stand in the judgment, nor sinners in the congregation of the righteous. For the LORD knoweth the way of the righteous: but the way of the ungodly shall perish.

Psalm 1:1-6

Prayer for Your Children

Arise, cry out in the night: in the beginning of the watches pour out thine heart like water before the face of the Lord: lift up thy hands toward him for the life of thy young children,...

Lamentations 2:19

Walk in a manner worthy of the calling with which you have been called, with all humility and gentleness, with patience, showing tolerance for one another in love, being diligent to preserve the unity of the Spirit in the bond of peace. There is one body and one Spirit, just as also you were called in one hope of your calling; one Lord, one faith, one baptism, one God and Father of all who is over all and through all and in all.

Ephesians 4:1-6 (NASB)

Now may God give you of the dew of heaven, And of the fatness of the earth, And an abundance of grain and new wine; May peoples serve you, And nations bow down to you; …Cursed be those who curse you, And blessed be those who bless you."

Genesis 27:28-29 (NASB)

That the God of our Lord Jesus Christ, the Father of glory, may give unto you the spirit of wisdom and revelation in the knowledge of him: The eyes of your understanding being enlightened; that ye may know what is the hope of his calling, and what the riches of the glory of his inheritance in the saints, And what is the exceeding greatness of his power to us-ward who believe, according to the working of his mighty power.

Ephesians 1:17-19

For we are his workmanship, created in Christ Jesus unto good works, which God hath before ordained that we should walk in them.

Ephesians 2:10

And all thy children shall be taught of the LORD; and great shall be the peace of thy children. In righteousness shalt thou be established: thou shalt be far from oppression; for thou shalt not fear: and from terror; for it shall not come near thee.

Isaiah 54:13-14

"No weapon that is formed against you will prosper; And every tongue that accuses you in judgment you will condemn. This is the heritage of the servants of the LORD, and their vindication is from Me," declares the LORD.

Isaiah 54:17 (NASB)

Thy testimonies are wonderful: therefore doth my soul keep them. The entrance of thy words giveth light; it giveth understanding unto the simple. I opened my mouth, and panted: for I longed for thy commandments. Look thou upon me, and be merciful unto me, as thou usest to do unto those that love thy name. Order my steps in thy word: and let not any iniquity have dominion over me. Deliver me from the oppression of man: so will I keep thy precepts. Make thy face to shine upon thy servant; and teach me thy statutes.

Psalm 119:129-135

He that dwelleth in the secret place of the most High shall abide under the shadow of the Almighty. I will say of the LORD, He is my refuge and my fortress: my God; in him will I trust. Surely he shall deliver thee from the snare of the fowler, and from the noisome pestilence. He shall cover thee with his feathers, and under his wings shalt thou trust: his truth shall be thy shield and buckler. Thou shalt not be afraid for the terror by night; nor for the arrow that flieth by day; Nor for the pestilence that walketh in darkness; nor for the destruction that wasteth at noonday. A thousand shall fall at thy side, and ten thousand at thy right hand; but it shall not come nigh thee. Only with thine eyes shalt thou behold and see the reward of the wicked. Because thou hast made the LORD, which is my refuge, even the most High, thy habitation; There shall no evil befall thee, neither shall any plague come nigh thy dwelling. For he shall give his angels charge over thee, to keep thee in all thy ways. They shall bear thee up in their hands, lest thou dash thy foot against a stone. Thou shalt tread upon the lion and adder: the young lion and the dragon shalt thou trample under feet. Because he hath set his love upon me, therefore will I deliver him: I will set him on high, because he hath known my name. He shall call upon me, and I will answer him: I will be with him in trouble; I will deliver him, and honour him. With long life will I satisfy him, and shew him my salvation.

Psalm 91:1-16

Establish my footsteps in Your word, And do not let any iniquity have dominion over me.

Psalm 119:133 (NASB)

Prayer for Your Family and Church Family

For this cause we also, since the day we heard it, do not cease to pray for you, and to desire that ye might be filled with the knowledge of his will in all wisdom and spiritual understanding; That ye might walk worthy of the Lord unto all pleasing, being fruitful in every good work, and increasing in the knowledge of God; Strengthened with all might, according to his glorious power, unto all patience and longsuffering with joyfulness; Giving thanks unto the Father, which hath made us meet to be partakers of the inheritance of the saints in light: Who hath delivered us from the power of darkness, and hath translated us into the kingdom of his dear Son:

Colossians 1:9-13

For this cause I bow my knees unto the Father of our Lord Jesus Christ, Of whom the whole family in heaven and earth is named, That he would grant you, according to the riches of his glory, to be strengthened with might by his Spirit in the inner man; That Christ may dwell in your hearts by faith; that ye, being rooted and grounded in love, May be able to comprehend with all saints what is the breadth, and length, and depth, and height; And to know the love of Christ, which passeth knowledge, that ye might be filled with all the fullness of God. Now unto him that is able to do exceeding abundantly above all that we ask or think, according to the power that worketh in us, Unto him be glory in the church by Christ Jesus throughout all ages, world without end. Amen.

Ephesians 3:14-21

And this I pray, that your love may abound yet more and more in knowledge and in all judgment; That ye

may approve things that are excellent; that ye may
be sincere and without offence till the day of Christ;
Being filled with the fruits of righteousness, which
are by Jesus Christ, unto the glory and praise of God.
Philippians 1:9-11

And now, Lord, behold their threatenings: and grant
unto thy servants, that with all boldness they may
speak thy word, By stretching forth thine hand to heal;
and that signs and wonders may be done by the name
of thy holy child Jesus. And when they had prayed,
the place was shaken where they were assembled
together; and they were all filled with the Holy Ghost,
and they spake the word of God with boldness.
Acts 4:29-31

Cease not to give thanks for you, making mention of
you in my prayers; That the God of our Lord Jesus
Christ, the Father of glory, may give unto you the spirit
of wisdom and revelation in the knowledge of him: The
eyes of your understanding being enlightened; that ye
may know what is the hope of his calling, and what the
riches of the glory of his inheritance in the saints, And
what is the exceeding greatness of his power to us-ward
who believe, according to the working of his mighty
power, Which he wrought in Christ, when he raised him
from the dead, and set him at his own right hand in the
heavenly places, Far above all principality, and power,
and might, and dominion, and every name that is named,
not only in this world, but also in that which is to come:
And hath put all things under his feet, and gave him to
be the head over all things to the church, Which is his
body, the fulness of him that filleth all in all.
Ephesians 1:16-23

PASSAGES TO LEARN AS A FAMILY

The Lord's Prayer

After this manner therefore pray ye:
Our Father which art in heaven,
Hallowed be thy name.
Thy kingdom come.
Thy will be done in earth, as it is in heaven.
Give us this day our daily bread.
And forgive us our debts, as we forgive our debtors.
And lead us not into temptation, but deliver us from evil:
For thine is the kingdom, and the power, and the glory, for ever. Amen.

Matthew 6:9-13

The Golden Rule

Therefore all things whatsoever ye would that men
should do to you,
Do ye even so to them: for this is the law and the
prophets.

Matthew 7:12

The Beatitudes

Blessed are the poor in spirit: for theirs is the kingdom of heaven.

Blessed are they that mourn: for they shall be comforted.

Blessed are the meek: for they shall inherit the earth.

Blessed are they which do hunger and thirst after righteousness: for they shall be filled.

Blessed are the merciful: for they shall obtain mercy.

Blessed are the pure in heart: for they shall see God.

Blessed are the peacemakers: for they shall be called the children of God.

Blessed are they which are persecuted for righteousness' sake: for theirs is the kingdom of heaven.

Blessed are ye, when men shall revile you, and persecute you, and shall say all manner of Evil against you falsely, for my sake.

Rejoice, and be exceeding glad: for great is your reward in heaven: for so persecuted they the prophets which were before you.

Matthew 5:3-12

The Ten Commandments

Thou shalt have no other gods before me.
Thou shalt not make unto thee any graven image.
Thou shalt not take God's name in vain;
Remember the Sabbath day, to keep it holy.
Honour thy father and thy mother
Thou shalt not kill.
Thou shalt not commit adultery.
Thou shalt not steal.
Thou shalt not bear false witness.
Thou shalt not covet.

Exodus 20:3-17

The Great Commandment

Master, which is the great commandment in the law?
Jesus said unto him,
Thou shalt love the Lord thy God with all thy heart,
and with all thy soul, and with all thy mind.
This is the first and great commandment.
And the second is like unto it, Thou shalt love thy
neighbour as thyself.
On these two commandments hang all the law and the
prophets.

Matthew 22:35-40

The Great Commission

And he said unto them, Go ye into all the world, and preach the gospel to every creature.

He that believeth and is baptized shall be saved; but he that believeth not shall be damned. And these signs shall follow them that believe;

In my name shall they cast out devils; they shall speak with new tongues; They shall take up serpents; and if they drink any deadly thing, it shall not hurt them; they shall lay hands on the sick, and they shall recover.

So then after the Lord had spoken unto them, he was received up into heaven, and sat on the right hand of God. And they went forth, and preached every where, the Lord working with them, and confirming the word with signs following. Amen.

Mark 16:15-20

The Twenty-Third Psalm

The LORD is my shepherd; I shall not want.
He maketh me to lie down in green pastures:
He leadeth me beside the still waters.
He restoreth my soul: he leadeth me in the paths of righteousness for his name's sake.
Yea, though I walk through the valley of the shadow of death, I will fear no evil: for thou art with me; thy rod and thy staff they comfort me.
Thou preparest a table before me in the presence of mine enemies: thou anointest my head with oil; my cup runneth over.
Surely goodness and mercy shall follow me all the days of my life: and I will dwell in the house of the LORD for ever.

Psalm 23:1-6

THE LIVING GOD

Some of the Descriptive Names of God

*K*nowing *the different names of God, as reflected in the Old and New Testaments, is a worshipful experience. It brings us closer to Him, to know who He is, and to love Him more.*

El Chai (Hai) "The Living God"
(Deut. 5:25, 26) (Rev. 1:18)

El Hannun "The Merciful God"
(Deut. 4:31) (John 8:10,11)

Jehovah Tzadekenu "The Lord Our Righteousness"
(Jer. 23:6) (Rom. 4:6, 24)

Jehovah Rohi "The Lord My Shepherd"
(Ps. 23:1) (John 10:14,15)

Jehovah Nissi "The Lord My Banner"
(Ex. 17:15) (Heb. 12:2)

Jehovah Jireth "The Lord Who Provides"
(Gen. 22:14) (Matt. 6:33)

Jehovah Rope "The Lord Who Heals You"
(Ex. 15:26) (John 9:1-7)

Jehovah Shalom "The Lord Is Peace"
(Judg. 6:24) (John 14:27)

El Kanna "The Jealous God"
(Ex. 20:5) (John 2:13-17)

El Abraham Yitzak v-Yacov "The God of Abraham, Isaac
and Jacob"
(Ex. 3:15). (John 8:38,39)

Names and Titles of Jesus Christ

The theme of the Bible is Jesus Christ and the redemption of mankind. Each book in the Holy Word clearly reveals Christ.

Jesus Christ, the same yesterday, and today, and for ever. Hebrews 13:8

GENESIS: The Ram of Sacrifice on Abraham's altar
EXODUS: The Passover Lamb
LEVITICUS: Our Atonement
NUMBERS: Our Guide
DEUTERONOMY: Our Refuge
JOSHUA: Rahab's Scarlet Cord
JUDGES: Our Judge
RUTH: Our Kinsman Redeemer
1 & 2 SAMUEL: The Trusted Prophet
KINGS and CHRONICLES: Our King
EZRA: The Faithful Scribe
NEHEMIAH: The Rebuilder
ESTHER: The Intercessor
JOB: Redeemer that Ever Liveth
PSALMS: Our Shepherd
PROVERBS and ECCLESIASTES: Our Wisdom
SONG OF SOLOMON: The Beautiful Bridegroom
ISAIAH: Our Sure Foundation
JEREMIAH: Our Hope
LAMENTATIONS: The Weeping Prophet
EZEKIEL: The Leader of God's people
DANIEL: The Fourth Man in the Midst of the Fiery Furnace
HOSEA: The Faithful Lover
JOEL: The Holy Spirit

OBADIAH: Our Avenger
JONAH: The Messenger of God's Word
MICAH: The Promised One
NAHUM: The Comforter
HABAKKUK: Omniscient God
ZEPHANIAH: The Lord Mighty to Save
HAGGAI: Desire of all Nations
ZECHARIAH: The Fountain for sin
MALACHI: The Sun of Righteousness with Healing in His Wings
MATTHEW: The Son of the Living God
MARK: The Healer and Miracle Worker
LUKE: Light of the Gentiles
JOHN: The Door
ACTS: Baptizer in The Holy Spirit
ROMANS: Our Justifier
1 CORINTHIANS: Abounding Love
2 CORINTHIANS: Forgiver of Sins
GALATIANS: Yoke Breaker
EPHESIANS: Our Inheritance
PHILIPPIANS: Our Provider
COLOSSIANS: Our Completeness in Him and
Our Hope in Death
1 & 2 THESSALONIANS: Our Soon Returning King
1 TIMOTHY: Immortal King
2 TIMOTHY: Our Victory
TITUS: Our Blessed Hope
PHILEMON: Loyal Friend
HEBREWS: Author and Finisher of Our Faith
JAMES: Our Healer
1 & 2 PETER: The Chief Shepherd
1 JOHN: Word of Life
2 JOHN: Our Love
3 JOHN: The Truth
JUDE: Our Lord Returning with 10,000 Saints

REVELATION: He is the King of kings and Lord of lords, He is Alpha and Omega.

Names and titles of Jesus

Advocate	1 John 2:1
Almighty	Revelation 1:8
Alpha and Omega	Revelation1:8, 11, 22:13
Anointed of the Lord	Psalm 2:2
Author and Finisher of Faith	Hebrews 12:2
Author of Eternal Salvation	Hebrews 5:9
Beginning and End	Revelation 1:8 &11
Beginning of Creation of God	Revelation3:14
Beloved Son	Matthew3:17, 2Peter 1:17
Bread from Heaven	John 6:51
Bread Of Life	John 6:48
Bridegroom	Matthew 9:15
Brightness of Father's Glory	Hebrews 1:3
Brother	Mark 3:35, Hebrews 2:11
Chief Shepherd	1Peter 5:4
Christ the Son of God	Acts 9:20
Cornerstone	Ephesians 2:20, 1Peter 2:6
Counselor	Isaiah 9:6
Day-Spring from on High	Luke 1:78
Day-Star	2 Peter 1:19
Deliverer	Romans 11:26
Desire of all Nations	Haggai 2:7
Diadem	Isaiah 28:5
Door of the Sheep	John 10:7 & 9
Emmanuel	Isaiah 7:14; Matthew 1:23
Eternal Life	1 John 5:20
Everlasting Father	Isaiah 9:6

Firstborn of every Creature	Colossians 1:15
First and Last	Revelation 1:11
Forerunner	Hebrews 6:20
Foundation laid in Zion	Isaiah 28:16
Fountain for Sin	Zechariah 13:1
Friend	Matthew 11:19
Gift of God	John 4:10, 2 Corinthians 9:15
Glorious Lord	Isaiah 33:21
Glory of God	Isaiah 40:5
God's Dear Son	Colossians 1:13
Good Teacher	Mark 10:17
Head of the Church	Ephesians 5:23; Colossians 1:18
Head over all Things	Hebrews 1:2
High Priest	Hebrews 3:1, 6:20, 7:26
Holy Child	Acts 4:30
Holy One of God	Mark 1:24
Holy One of Israel	Isaiah 41:14
Hope	Acts 28:20; 1 Timothy 1:1
Hope of Glory	Colossians 1:27
I Am	John 8:58
Image of the Invisible God	Colossians 1:15
Immortal	1 Timothy 1:17
Jesus of Nazareth	Mark 1:24; Luke 24:19
Jesus the Son of God	Hebrews 4:14
King of Glory	Psalm 24:7 & 10
King of Jews	Mark 15:26; Luke 23:38
King of Kings	Revelation 17:14

King over all the Earth . . . . Zechariah 14:9
Lamb of God . . . . John 1:29 & 36
Light of the World . . . . John 8:12; 9:5
Lily of the Valleys . . . . Song of Solomon 2:1
Lion of the Tribe of Judah . . . . Revelation 5:5
Living Bread . . . . John 6:51
Living Stone . . . . 1 Peter 2
Lord and Savior Jesus Christ . . . . 2 Peter 1:1; 3:18
Lord of All . . . . Acts 10:36
Lord of Lords . . . . Revelation 17:14; 19:16
Lord of the Dead and Living . . . . Romans 14:9
Lord Strong and Mighty . . . . Psalm 24:8
Lord our Righteousness . . . . Jeremiah 23:6
Lord your Holy One . . . . Isaiah 43:15
Lord your Redeemer . . . . Isaiah 43:14
Man of Sorrows . . . . Isaiah 53:3
Master . . . . Matthew 8:19; John 13:13
Mediator . . . . 1 Timothy 2:5; Hebrews 9:15
Merciful and Faithful . . . . Hebrews 2:17
Messiah . . . . Daniel 9:25; John 1:41; 4:25
Mighty One of Israel . . . . Isaiah 30:29
Morning Star . . . . Revelation 22:16
Most Holy . . . . Daniel 9:24
Nazarene . . . . Matthew 2:23
Only Begotten . . . . John 1:14
Our Peace . . . . Ephesians 2:14
Passover of the Saints . . . . 1 Corinthians 5:7

Pearl of Great Price. . . . . Matthew 13:46

Physician. . . . . Matthew 9:12

Power of God . . . . 1 Corinthians
1:24

Priest. . . . . Hebrews 5:6

Prince of Peace . . . . Isaiah 9:6

Prophet . . . . Luke 24:19;
Acts 3:22-23

Quickening Spirit . . . . 1 Corinthians
15:45

Rabbi. . . . . Matthew 26:25
& 49

Rain and Showers . . . . Psalm 72:6

Ransom for All . . . . 1 Timothy 2:6

Resurrection and the Life . . . . John 11:25

Righteous Servant. . . . . Isaiah 53:11

Rivers of Water. . . . . Isaiah 32:2

Rock of Offence . . . . Isaiah 8:14;
1 Peter 2:8

Rose of Sharon . . . . Song of
Solomon 2:1

Ruler of the Kings of the Earth. . . . . Revelation 1:5

Salvation. . . . . Luke 2:30

Savior of the World. . . . . John 4:42;
1 John 4:14

Sharp Sword . . . . Isaiah 49:2

Shepherd of the Souls . . . . 1 Peter 2:25

Spiritual Drink . . . . 1 Corinthians
10:4

Spiritual Meat . . . . 1 Corinthians
10:3

Spiritual Rock. . . . . 1 Corinthians
10:4

Son of the Most High . . . . Luke 1:31

Sure Foundation . . . . Isaiah 28:16

GOD'S WORD: LIFE-CHANGING

Where Will You Spend Eternity?

There is a Heaven! There is a Hell! You Choose Your Destination!

Heaven

The LORD hath prepared his throne in the heavens; and his kingdom ruleth over all.

Psalm 103:19

And I heard a great voice out of heaven saying, Behold, the tabernacle of God is with men, and he will dwell with them, and they shall be his people, and God himself shall be with them, and be their God. And God shall wipe away all tears from their eyes; and there shall be no more death, neither sorrow, nor crying, neither shall there be any more pain: for the former things are passed away.

Revelation 21:3-4

And he carried me away in the spirit to a great and high mountain, and shewed me that great city, the holy Jerusalem, descending out of heaven from God, Having the glory of God: and her light was like unto a

191

stone most precious, even like a jasper stone, clear as crystal; And had a wall great and high, and had twelve gates, and at the gates twelve angels, and names written thereon, which are the names of the twelve tribes of the children of Israel: On the east three gates; on the north three gates; on the south three gates; and on the west three gates. And the wall of the city had twelve foundations, and in them the names of the twelve apostles of the Lamb. And he that talked with me had a golden reed to measure the city, and the gates thereof, and the wall thereof. And the city lieth foursquare, and the length is as large as the breadth: and he measured the city with the reed, twelve thousand furlongs. The length and the breadth and the height of it are equal. And he measured the wall thereof, an hundred and forty and four cubits, according to the measure of a man, that is, of the angel. And the building of the wall of it was of jasper: and the city was pure gold, like unto clear glass. And the foundations of the wall of the city were garnished with all manner of precious stones. The first foundation was jasper; the second, sapphire; the third, a chalcedony; the fourth, an emerald; The fifth, sardonyx; the sixth, sardius; the seventh, chrysolite; the eighth, beryl; the ninth, a topaz; the tenth, a chrysoprasus; the eleventh, a jacinth; the twelfth, an amethyst. And the twelve gates were twelve pearls; every several gate was of one pearl: and the street of the city was pure gold, as it were transparent glass. And I saw no temple therein: for the Lord God Almighty and the Lamb are the temple of it. And the city had no need of the sun, neither of the moon, to shine in it: for the glory of God did lighten it, and the Lamb is the light thereof. And the nations of them which are saved shall walk in the light of it: and the kings of the earth do bring their glory and honour into it. And the gates of it shall not be shut at all by day: for there shall be no night there. And they shall bring the glory and honour of the nations into it.

Revelation 21:10-26

Nevertheless we, according to his promise, look for new heavens and a new earth, wherein dwelleth righteousness.

2 Peter 3:13

Hell

In flaming fire taking vengeance on them that know not God, and that obey not the gospel of our Lord Jesus Christ: Who shall be punished with everlasting destruction from the presence of the Lord, and from the glory of his power;

Thessalonians 1:8-9

But the heavens and the earth, which are now, by the same word are kept in store, reserved unto fire against the day of judgment and perdition of ungodly men.

2 Peter 3:7

But the fearful, and unbelieving, and the abominable, and murderers, and whoremongers, and sorcerers, and idolaters, and all liars, shall have their part in the lake which burneth with fire and brimstone: which is the second death.

Revelation 21:8

And whosoever was not found written in the book of life was cast into the lake of fire.

Revelation 20:15

The Plan of Salvation

1. Admit you have sinned. We all have sinned and need a Savior.

> For all have sinned, and come short of the glory of God;
>
> Romans 3:23

> If we say that we have no sin, we deceive ourselves, and the truth is not in us.
>
> 1 John 1:8

> For what shall it profit a man, if he shall gain the whole world, and lose his own soul? Or what shall a man give in exchange for his soul?
>
> Mark 8:36-37

2. Believe in the Savior Jesus Christ.

> For God so loved the world, that he gave his only begotten Son, that whosoever believeth in him should not perish, but have everlasting life.
>
> John 3:16

> But if we walk in the light, as he is in the light, we have fellowship one with another, and the blood of Jesus Christ his Son cleanseth us from all sin.
>
> 1 John 1:7

> ....Sirs, what must I do to be saved? And they said, Believe on the Lord Jesus Christ, and thou shalt be saved, and thy house.
>
> Acts 16:30-31

For the wages of sin is death; but the gift of God is eternal life through Jesus Christ our Lord.

Romans 6:23

Jesus saith unto him, I am the way, the truth, and the life: no man cometh unto the Father, but by me.

John 14:6

3. Confess with your mouth that Jesus Christ is Lord.

That if thou shalt confess with thy mouth the Lord Jesus, and shalt believe in thine heart that God hath raised him from the dead, thou shalt be saved. For whosoever shall call upon the name of the Lord shall be saved.

Romans 10:9 & 13

For with the heart man believeth unto righteousness; and with the mouth confession is made unto salvation.

Romans 10:10

If we confess our sins, he is faithful and just to forgive us our sins, and to cleanse us from all unrighteousness.

1 John 1:9

4. Confess your sins to God and repent of your sins.

I tell you, Nay: but, except ye repent, ye shall all likewise perish.

Luke 13:3

But if we walk in the Light as He Himself is in the Light, we have fellowship with one another, and the blood of Jesus His Son cleanses us from all sin.

1 John 1:7 (NASB)

Repent ye therefore, and be converted, that your sins may be blotted out, when the times of refreshing shall come from the presence of the Lord;

Acts 3:19

Behold, I stand at the door, and knock: if any man hear my voice, and open the door, I will come in to him, and will sup with him, and he with me.

Revelation 3:20

Sinner's Prayer

Father God in heaven, I repent of all my sins.
I ask You to forgive me and cleanse me of all my
unrighteousness
with Your Son's blood.
I confess with my mouth and believe in my heart that
You raised Jesus from the dead.
I accept Jesus Christ as my own personal Lord and
Savior.
I believe Your Word.
I now have eternal life, a free gift of God.
Thank You, Jesus, for dying on the cross for me
and for giving me a new life.
Help me to live a life that will bring glory to Your name.

Amen.

Empowering Daily Confession

I believe in confessing what God says about me in the Bible. That's why I am sharing with you my daily confession.

We must believe and say what we want to see happen in our life instead of dwelling in what we are facing right now.

When we confess of who we are in Christ, we are not glorifying ourselves, but honoring God for what He has done for us and in us through His Son, Jesus Christ.

God loves us and wants to bless us in every way. He gave His Son Jesus, who gave His life, that we might become God's children and enjoy all the blessings of His family.

What God has legally provided through Christ becomes ours by believing what He said in His Word and by confessing them with our mouth.

If we want things to change in our life, we need to move our mouth so things will move toward the right direction.

Agree with God by saying what He says about you in the Bible, and you will see things begin to change in your life.

I confess with your mouth, "Jesus is Lord," and believe in my heart that God raised him from the dead.

I am a child of God; a coheir with Christ, inheriting His Glory.

I am justified as a gift by His grace through the redemption which is in Christ Jesus.

I am a new creation: The old has gone, the new is here!

God has given me a new heart and put a new spirit in me; He has removed my heart of stone and gave me a heart of flesh.

Christ has redeemed me from the curse of the law by becoming a curse for me.

I am born again, not of perishable seed, but of imperishable, through the living and enduring word of God.

I praise You Father that I am amazingly and wonderfully made. What you have done is wonderful. I know that very well.

I am a chosen generation, a royal priesthood, an holy nation, a peculiar people; that I should shew forth the praises of him who hath called me out of darkness into his marvelous light;

I have been crucified with Christ and I no longer live, but Christ lives in me. The life I live in the body, I live by faith in the Son of God, who loved me and gave himself for me.

I am the temple of the Holy Ghost and God's property and possession.

I am blessed with all spiritual blessings in heavenly places.

I abound in wisdom, insight, and understanding.

I have God-like faith to speak into existence with my mouth those things that I believe in my heart.

I can agree with another in prayer and receive anything I ask.

My husband and I are one flesh. God has joined us together so we will live in unity.

Our marriage is exciting and fulfilling because my husband loves me as Christ loves the church and I reverence my husband and submits to his headship in our marriage.

My husband and I love each other deeply, because love covers over a multitude of sins.

My children obey and honor me so it will go well with them, and they will live long on earth.

I am blessed in the city and blessed in the field. I am a blessing going in and a blessing going out. Everything I put my hands to will be blessed. I will lend and not borrow. I am the head and not the tail. I am always at the top never at the bottom.

I am God's handiwork, created in Christ, to do His work.

I will not become weary in doing good, for at the proper time I will reap a harvest if I do not give up.

I have the mind of Christ. He has given me His wisdom to make right choices. God has generously given me His wisdom.

The LORD will bless me and will keep me;

He will make His face shine on me and will be gracious to me;

He will turn His face toward me and give me peace;

And He will bless me.

I will approach the throne of grace with confidence, so that I may receive mercy and find grace to help me in my time of need.

And my God will meet all my needs according to his glorious riches in Christ Jesus.

I have no fear of lack for my life because my Father God owns everything. For every animal of the forest is mine, and the cattle on a thousand hills.

My God is able to do exceeding abundantly above all that I ask or think, according to the power that is working in me.

I can do all things through Christ who gives me strength.

I always triumph in Christ. I am the manifest fragrance of His knowledge in every place.

But whatever was to my profit I now consider loss for the sake of Christ. What is more, I consider everything a loss compared to the surpassing greatness of knowing Christ Jesus my Lord, for whose sake I have lost all things. I consider them rubbish, that I may gain Christ and be found in him, not having a righteousness of my own that comes from the law, but that which is through faith in Christ—the righteousness that comes from God and is by faith. I want to know Christ and the power of his resurrection and the fellowship of sharing in his sufferings, becoming like him in his death, and so, somehow, to attain to the resurrection from the dead. Not that I have already obtained all this, or have already been made perfect, but I press on to take hold of that for which Christ Jesus took hold of me. I do not consider myself yet to have taken hold of it. But one thing I do: Forgetting what is behind and straining toward what is ahead, I press on toward the goal to win the prize for which God has called me heavenward in Christ Jesus.

I will not fear because God, who takes hold of my right hand and says to me, Do not fear; I will help you.

For God did not give me a spirit of timidity, but a spirit of power, of love and of self-discipline.

I have everlasting consolation, encouragement, and hope.

I have the peace of God, which transcends all understanding, (and) will guard my heart and my mind in Christ Jesus.

I am filled with the knowledge of God's will in all wisdom and spiritual understanding.

I am fruitful in every good work; I am increasing in the knowledge of God.

I am strengthened by His glorious power for patience, longsuffering, and joyfulness.

God will also make me a light for the Gentiles, that I may bring God's salvation to the ends of the earth." This is what the LORD says— ..."Kings will see me and rise up, princes will see and bow down, because of the LORD, who is faithful, the Holy One of Israel, who has chosen me." This is what the LORD says: "In the time of my favor I will answer you, and in the day of salvation I will help you; I will keep you and will make you to be a covenant for the people, to restore the land and to reassign its desolate inheritances, to say to the captives, 'Come out,' and to those in darkness, 'Be free!'

I will not rise early and stay up late, toiling for food to eat— because God loves me He gives me a good night's rest.

God raised me...up for this very purpose that God might display His power in me that God's name might be proclaimed in all the earth."

What, then, shall we say in response to these things? If God is for us, who can be against us?

I give so it will be given to me; A good measure, pressed down, shaken together and running over, will be poured into my lap. For with the measure I use, it will be measured to me.

I am a faithful person so I will be richly blessed,

I have a rich and satisfying life in Christ Jesus.

God answers me before I even call to Him. While I am still talking about my needs, He will go ahead and answer my prayers!

I will lift up mine eyes unto the hills, from whence cometh my help. My help cometh from the LORD, which made heaven and earth.

I have set the LORD always before me: because he is at my right hand, I shall not be moved. Therefore my heart is glad, and my glory rejoiceth: my flesh also shall rest in hope. It is God that girdeth me with strength, and maketh my way perfect. He maketh my feet like hinds' feet, and setteth me upon my high places.

I am confident God will perfect His work in me. I abound in love to know and discern. I am able to know what is best, that I might be untainted and pure. I am being filled with the fruit of righteousness for God's glory.

I pray according to God's will in the Spirit, and all things work together for my good. God is for me, and no one can effectively be against me.

I am more than a conqueror in any circumstance adverse to my well-being.

Nothing can separate me from God's love, which is in Christ Jesus our Lord.

I will obey and serve God, so I will spend the rest of my life in prosperity and my years in contentment.

I will call on God and He will answer me: He will be with me in trouble; He will deliver me and honor me. He will satisfy me with long life and will show me His salvation.

I believe the Words of Jesus so I will see the glory of God.

I make confession with my lips unto health, preservation, deliverance, safety, and soundness in my life and my family.

I will be careful to live a blameless life. I will lead a life of integrity in my own home.

I will refuse to look at anything vile and vulgar.

I will fight the good fight of faith, take hold of the eternal life to which I am called, and I will make the good confession in the presence of many witnesses.

I am uncompromisingly righteous so I will flourish like the palm tree. I will live long, dignified, upright, useful and fruitful. I will grow like a cedar in Lebanon, majestic, stable, durable and incorruptible. I will be planted in the house of the Lord, flourishing in the courts of my God. I will grow in grace and bring fruit in old age; I will be full of sap of spiritual vitality and rich in the verdure. I will be a living memorial to show that the Lord is upright and faithful to His promises.

And this is the confidence that we have in him, that, if we ask any thing according to his will, he hears us:

And if we know that he hear us, whatsoever we ask, we know that we have the petitions that we desired of him.

Scripture references: Empowering Daily Confession

Romans 10:9
John 1:12; Romans 8:17
Romans 3:24
2 Corinthians 5:17
Ezekiel 36:26
Galatians 3:13
1 Peter 1:23
Psalm 139:14
1 Peter 2:9
Galatians 2:20
1 Corinthians 6:19-20
Ephesians 1:3
Ephesians 1:8
Mark 11:24
Matthew 18:19
Matthew 19:6
Ephesians 5:25 & 33
1 Peter 4:8
Ephesians 6:1-3
Deuteronomy 28:3 & 6, 12-13
Ephesians 2:10
Galatians 6:9
1 Corinthians 2:16; James 1:5
Numbers 6:24-27
Hebrews 4:16
Philippians 4:19
Psalm 50:10
Ephesians 3:20
Philippians 4:13
1 Corinthians 2:14
Philippians 3:7-14
Isaiah 41:13
2 Timothy 1:7

2 Thessalonians 2:16
Philippians 4:7
Colossians 1:9-11
Isaiah 49:6-9
Psalm 127:2
Romans 9:17
Romans 8:31
Luke 6:38
Proverbs 28:20
John 10:10
Isaiah 65:24
Psalm 121:1-2
Psalm 18:32-33
Philippians 1:6-11
Romans 8:26-28 & 31
Romans 8:37-39
Job 36:11
Psalm 91:15-16
Romans 10:10
Psalm 101:2-3
1 Timothy 6:12
Psalm 92:12-15
1 John 5:14-15

Dear Friends,

When you purchase "Secret for a Successful Day," you will be helping to translate and to send it to other nations as the Lord opens the doors.

Thank you, and may The Lord Jesus Christ bless you abundantly as you sow into His Kingdom.

Alemla Zwahr

Write to:
P.O. Box 387
Guy, Texas 77444-0387

I would like to thank the anonymous person whose generous donation has funded the second print run. May the God of abundance give you many returns on your investment!

CPSIA information can be obtained at www.ICGtesting.com
Printed in the USA
LVOW100702170313

324573LV00001B/1/P